I0803046

Praise for

BECAUSE THEY NEED US

"*Because They Need Us* is not a collection of anecdotes about someone's past accomplishments as much as it is a road map. It's an ethical road map, a life road, a road map for success! Like all of Judie's efforts, it's replete with passion, moral conviction, and a sense of purpose."

—**ANTHONY RENDON,** speaker emeritus of the California Assembly

"*Because They Need Us* is a powerful account of how things get done in government when armed with boundless energy, moral conviction, and perseverance—even when facing mountainous, well-funded opposition. It's no surprise that morally flexible legislators and unscrupulous lobbyists are on edge when Judie walks into a room. They know her moral conviction on behalf of our beloved animals runs far deeper than the surface nature of transactional politics."

—**ASH KALRA,** California State Assemblymember and compassionate vegan

"Judie Mancuso is a Joan of Arc for animals, a force that, as you will read, could not be bought for a million dollars. Why are pet shops banned from selling puppy mill pups? Judie is the reason. Woe to any special interest groups that think they can outspend and outsmart Judie. Almost anything to do with animal protection in the state of California is because of her and her devoted team of vigorous animal defenders. *Because They Need Us* is eye-opening and jaw-dropping, revealing the lobbyists' games as well as the commitment and determination it takes to defeat them."

—**INGRID NEWKIRK,** bestselling author and founder and president of People for the Ethical Treatment of Animals (PETA)

"*Because They Need Us* is a brilliantly written blow-by-blow account of the grit and political smarts it takes to defeat huge corporate forces in the name of decency and compassion. This book could be a textbook for anyone who aims to change the world, as Judie Mancuso has masterfully done."

—**DR. NEAL D. BARNARD,** author, psychiatrist, and founding president of the Physicians Committee for Responsible Medicine

"Judie Mancuso has been the singular driving force behind more than twenty truly groundbreaking pieces of animal rights legislation. *Because They Need Us* tells how she took on Goliath to get these landmark bills signed into law. Had you gone to Vegas and bet against the thousand-to-one odds of them passing, you would be on the Forbes 400 today. This book is a must-read."

—**DR. GARY MICHELSON,** founder and funder of the Michelson Found Animals Foundation

"Judie Mancuso is a force of nature! Her fast-paced political memoir reads like a thriller. Courageously standing up for animals, she refuses to be intimidated by the powerful, monied interests that come after her. A must-read!"

—**JANE VELEZ-MITCHELL,** *New York Times* bestselling author and president of UnchainedTV

"In the animal rights movement, few individuals are 'the real deal'—those who truly grasp the simple (yet too-often ignored) fact that animals are not ours to exploit and use. Judie has gone to war to fight giant corporations and industries that profit from harming animals. *Because They Need Us* is an inside look at what goes on in the trenches and how battles for animal rights are won."

—**SIMONE REYES,** world-renowned animal activist, TEDx speaker, author, and Social Compassion in Legislation board member

BECAUSE THEY NEED US

BECAUSE THEY NEED US

MY POLITICAL FIGHT TO SAVE ANIMALS

JUDIE MANCUSO

Because They Need Us: My Political Fight to Save Animals

Cover design by Kevin Olds
Special thanks to the Laguna Beach Cultural Arts Center

For more information, please contact:
Amplify Publishing, an imprint of Amplify Publishing Group
620 Herndon Parkway, Suite 220
Herndon, VA 20170
info@amplifypublishing.com

Library of Congress Control Number: 2024914685

CPSIA Code: PRFRE0824A

ISBN-13: 979-8-89138-345-6

Printed in the Canada

Printed on post-consumer waste paper

To all the voiceless animals that needlessly suffer and die because they lack protection: our hearts bleed for you, and our fight continues.

CONTENTS

PROLOGUE

The hotshot lobbyist representing the alligator skin industry swaggered in with a big used car salesman smile. Tall and lanky, exuding confidence, he was at the top of his game, a Grand Poobah in what's known in Sacramento as the "Third House"—the group of lobbyists who influence much of what happens in the California Assembly and Senate. He greeted us like old friends, but I knew he was deeply annoyed that some little animal rights group was getting in the way of his mission: his clients wanted all legal restrictions on imports and sales of alligator and crocodile skin products permanently removed in California. It was his job to make that happen.

The meeting was in the cafeteria in the basement of the old Capitol building. It's a long, narrow room with brick walls that have seen their share of dealmaking. I had my five lobbyists with me. We arrived first and filled a table for six directly in front of the entrance, squeezing a seventh chair in opposite me for the man who'd requested the meeting.

After minimal pleasantries, he cut to the chase.

"Judie, we need to get this bill passed."

"And we need to protect the alligators."

The conversation could have stopped there as far as I was concerned. I had better things to do, more votes to get to defeat the bill he was pushing. But my own lobbyists, professionals who had been active in the state legislature for decades, had made me promise to stay long enough to say I'd met with the other side.

"Tell him to read the thousands of letters from our supporters," I said. "That is our message."

"You don't know what *he's* going to say, though," my lead lobbyist, David, responded.

"I know exactly what he's going to say. He's going to ask us to sell out the alligators. The answer is no."

"Just let me arrange a meeting. You don't have to stay for long. And you don't have to agree to anything. It's good politics to say you at least heard the other side out."

He was right, of course. It *is* good politics. When you stand up to high-end fashion houses and factory farms and other animal exploiters, no matter what you say or do, you immediately get labeled an animal rights extremist. It's their playbook. These industries make hundreds of millions of dollars a year with business models that have cruelty written into them. Challenge their practices, and you challenge their profits. That's why they spare no cost in hiring the most ruthless lobbyists to make their case. Like the man I was sitting across from now.

His well-rehearsed speech was painful to listen to. Did we know that American alligators were no longer on the endangered species list thanks to the work of the Louisiana alligator industry? Yes, I knew that they were no longer considered endangered. Purely a business decision. You can't make money off animals that are extinct. What about all the conservation efforts that were being funded by the hide and meat industry? His clients had to preserve some wetlands so they would have a place to breed animals for slaughter. Also a financial decision. Dressing up the exploitation machine as conservation work—I'd heard every version of that pitch over the years. Industry profits never came up once, of course, even though that's the only thing he was there to protect. And not a word about the torture these animals endure. I didn't even bother going there. He knew exactly how his clients operated.

You don't have to be a big believer in animal rights like me to agree that what happens on alligator and crocodile farms is barbaric. These living beings are hatched in captivity, then packed shoulder to shoulder in dank, dark pits from the time they are born. They're kept there twenty-four hours a day, standing in fetid water with barely enough room to move. In the wild, alligators can live up to seventy years. On these farms, they're killed in the most disgusting way possible as soon as they're a year or two old. All to satisfy people's desire for expensive status symbols like alligator boots and wallets. And to quench the endless greed of the businesses making money off of their backs, literally, such as fashion houses and luxury retail stores.

Sales of alligator and crocodile products were banned in California in 1970. Public opinion overwhelmingly supported the ban. But lobbyists working on behalf of the state of Louisiana, breeders, hunters, fashion houses, and the retail industry had convinced California legislators to adopt a five-year exemption in 2005. It was supposed to be a one-time thing, but the exemption had been extended twice. The basement meeting took place before the summer of 2019, so six months before the exemption was to expire. The clock was ticking. If they couldn't get a bill passed before the end of the legislative session, the alligator skin industry would no longer have access to the massive California market.

Social Compassion in Legislation (SCIL), the nonprofit I founded in 2007, had acquired a reputation as a fearless defender of animals and something of a legislative powerhouse. Remember when pet stores in California had to stop buying animals from puppy mills and make shelter animals available for adoption instead? That was us. Did you know that since 2020, it's been illegal to sell cosmetics and personal hygiene products tested on animals in the Golden State? We did that too. Enjoy dining on restaurant patios with your dog in California? SCIL made it possible. In 2019, we were working around the clock to get even more landmark pro-animal bills through the legislature. But when we found out what the alligator skin industry was up to, we jumped into high gear and fought back.

The man we were meeting with in the cafeteria had seen what we were capable of. He knew we were powerful, and he knew we meant business.

"So, Judie, here's what I'm wondering. I know you and your nonprofit care about conservation as much as my clients do. At the end of the day, you want the same thing."

"Let me be clear: we do not want the same thing."

He smiled at me like I was an unruly child challenging him in an argument he was certain to win. He assumed it was just a matter of time.

"I think you're going to be interested in what I have to say. My clients want to set up a conservation fund with, say, half a million dollars in it. To start. Think about all those projects you're working on. How many animals you could save with that kind of money."

"What do the alligators get?"

That toothy smile again.

"You'd be able to use the money any way you want. And you yourself would be in charge of the fund. As executive director, you'd have full control over allocation. To save wetlands and wildlife and all the other things you care about. Think about it."

"That's not going to happen," I said. "Our goals are not aligned. In fact, they're opposite. I started my group to save animals, not to sell them out. It would go against my whole moral compass and every single thing we stand for to be bought off by your clients so that they can perpetuate their abuse. We're here for the animals. We are their voice."

"I understand that. And I laud your passion. But this is a lot of money we're talking about. And it could be more. What if my clients made it a million dollars? Now *that* would allow you to do some real good. You could share some of it with the other groups you work with. Let me just say it could change a lot of lives. Starting with yours."

Well, he wasn't wrong. A huge part of running a small but mighty nonprofit like SCIL is fundraising and scraping together funds to hire lobbyists and other professionals. Sometimes it feels like raising money is my real full-time job, one that keeps me from doing the actual work of getting laws passed to save animals. A million dollars would have made a world of difference. To us. But not to the alligators. And we were here for them.

"Unfortunately, there's nothing I can do to stop your clients from torturing and slaughtering animals. Believe me, if there was, I would do it. But I can sure try to keep them from bringing their heinous business into California."

This response was definitely not what he was expecting. Dispatched by his clients to get me to yes by offering what would for

SCIL be a monumental sum of money, he counted on us taking it and walking away. They pictured us rationalizing and justifying and telling ourselves that in the big picture, the deal was a win-win. A lot of groups would have accepted the offer. I've seen it happen time and time again. But not us, not SCIL.

He looked like he was weighing his next move. Perhaps his clients had authorized him to up the ante? To keep going until we caved? California is a huge market for the luxury retail industry. There was a lot at stake. Maybe the sky really was the limit. We'll never know because I ended the conversation right there.

"You can go as high as you want, the answer will still be no. There is no dollar amount that will turn this conversation around. Someone needs to speak for the animals. That someone is me. Until your clients change their ways, I'm not going to change mine."

Next thing I knew he was on his feet, slamming his chair under the table so hard that it shook, and charging off. My lobbyists had grins on their faces. They obviously had a whole David and Goliath movie playing in their heads and saw this as an epic moment. But they were also shocked to realize that I didn't have a point at which I'd bargain the animals away.

David, the lobbyist who had convinced me to attend this little rendezvous turned to me and said, "Well, Judie, you've made the big time. They only try to bribe you when they fear you."

■ ■ ■

I'd worked with rescues and animal causes for decades before I founded SCIL. Of course, there were moments of great joy and purpose during that time. But my overall experience was one of nonstop setbacks, heartaches, and exasperation at the absence of political will to take concrete action to protect animals, including through legislation. In 2007, in California, no one was addressing the systemic problems at a higher level: pet overpopulation and the lack of public funding for spay and neuter programs. All the industries with business models that require treating animals like non-sentient beings. The need for education about what meat and dairy consumption is doing to our bodies and to our planet.

A day came when I had to admit that I was probably the person I'd been waiting for. I had the temperament to get in the trenches and dig my heels in. I had wonderful animal-loving friends and supporters to back me up. And I had the passion. You can't do this work without a fire in your heart that burns for the animals.

So I set up a nonprofit to pass laws that protect animals and defeat ones that harm them, and I jumped in the water, figuring I'd learn to swim.

What I discovered is that it takes monumental effort to get even the most straightforward legislation passed. It takes months and even years to tell the story of why a law is necessary, the benefits it will offer, the money it will save, the animal suffering it will prevent . . . Behind the scenes, countless hours go into stroking lawmakers' egos, reassuring them that supporting a bill isn't going to land them in hot water with donors, their political party, or their constituents.

This is my story about learning how to navigate the California state legislature to pass landmark bills, when at times everyone—and I mean everyone—said it couldn't be done. My journey includes learning how to stand up to some of the biggest industries and special interests in the world, all in service of protecting animals. I'll talk about spineless politicians, fake animal welfare groups, and baffling legislative processes. But you'll also read about unprecedented successes in the animal rights space. In the end, my message is one of hope. We can make the world a more compassionate place for animals and humans. We can save the planet. You can be an integral part of that movement, no matter your background. Just find your niche and jump in.

When people ask why SCIL has been so successful, I tell them it's because I don't back down and I never go back on my word. My response to the guy representing the alligator killers? I'm like that all the time. It makes me a known quantity. People appreciate knowing exactly who they're dealing with. Ask anyone who's ever worked with me and SCIL, they'll all say the same thing: We're just here for the animals. To be the voice for the voiceless.

CHAPTER 1

THE POLITICAL EDUCATION OF JUDIE MANCUSO

In my home state of California, animal shelters were taking in over a million companion animals a year in 2007, and euthanizing more than half of them. These were animals that were lost, abandoned, or born on the street. Rescues and fosters could not begin to keep up. The numbers were just too big.

It was a devastating situation for the animals, and truly traumatic for shelter workers, rescue groups, and veterinarians. The state was spending close to $300 million a year, first to house and then to euthanize the animals they couldn't reunite with their families or adopt out. A lose-lose situation all around.

Pet overpopulation is a tragic, expensive problem. Spaying and neutering programs were key to solving it. Lawmakers were interested in finding solutions to problems, weren't they?

That was my naïve thinking going into my first legislative battle as sponsor and campaign director for the California Healthy Pets

Act, which would have mandated fixing most dogs and cats in California by the age of six months, with a long list of exceptions and carve-outs.

The campaign would be an eye-opening, heartbreaking crash course in politics. It gave me my first look behind the curtain at how bills get passed or killed because of special interests and cowardly lawmakers for whom making society better and saving taxpayers money are not top priorities.

One *Los Angeles Times* reporter who followed the battle closely wrote an article about it entitled "The Political Education of Judie Mancuso." Indeed.

And what an education it has been.

■ ■ ■

Widespread flooding after Hurricane Katrina left 80 percent of New Orleans underwater. Hundreds of thousands of families in the area owned pets at the time of the disaster. As they fled by any means possible to save their own lives, countless animals were left behind. There was no evacuation plan that included pets, and no system for keeping track of these pets if they were rescued. This lack of planning turned a natural disaster and humanitarian crisis into a pet crisis. In addition to the companion animals left to fend for themselves, the city was overrun with stray dogs and cats that had no source of food once the people were gone. Nearly all of them were unaltered, and they were producing more unowned animals every day. A perfect recipe for a catastrophe within a catastrophe.

My friend Jane Garrison was certified in disaster rescue, and she was among the first specialized animal rescuers to arrive in New Orleans to assist local animal control. She had set up operations inside the Lamar-Dixon Expo Center in Gonzales, Louisiana, between Baton Rouge and New Orleans. It had been transformed into an emergency relief center for displaced people and animals.

Almost immediately, the temporary animal shelter was overflowing. On days when space couldn't be made for more animals, volunteers would go door to door and simply leave food and water inside the homes where they found animals, hoping the owners would return. Sometimes they'd go back a few days later to find the animals dead.

It was early morning in California when Jane called, sobbing. She was wrapping up a long night of going house to house to save animals, with no end in sight. A rescuer's worst nightmare. Could I come join the effort on the ground? Please? There was an endless stream of animals coming in, not enough people to care for them, and no one to work specifically on reuniting them with their families.

I'd been deeply involved in rescue work for a decade at that point, and it was gradually becoming the center of my life. Standing by and watching this tragedy play out wasn't an option.

I recruited my friend and fellow rescue activist Priscilla to go to New Orleans with me. Jane had reached out to her too, and Priscilla also felt like she couldn't stay home. Within a few days, we were ready to start our journey. Making travel arrangements was complicated. The New Orleans airport was obviously closed. We flew into Houston and rented a Toyota 4Runner to drive the rest of the way. What should have been a six-hour trip took us eleven. All the hotels along our route were full, and many of the stores had no food. These businesses were catering to all the people fleeing the flooding as well as those going in to help with cleanup and rescue. Luckily, we had anticipated this, and packed enough essentials to keep us going for a week.

We ended up camping out in the 4Runner in the parking lot of one of the hotels that couldn't accommodate us. Sleeping in the car was not easy for Priscilla, with her five-foot-ten frame. Knowing we needed a few hours of rest, we moved the car within sight of the guard assigned to watch the parking lot for the night and placed all our luggage underneath it. It was the only way we could put the seats back.

The heat was stifling. Once the air conditioning was off, it was hard to breathe.

Neither of us had even been to a disaster zone before. It was truly daunting. I had seen images of the aftermath of the levee break with people being carried away by the water and Xs being placed on homes where bodies or animals had been found. Video of people on rooftops, waving desperately for help.

By the time we woke up, the fear was forgotten and we were in action mode. We went straight to Lamar-Dixon. The National Guard was posted at the entrance to this massive property, checking IDs. They confirmed that we were on the list of rescue volunteers and waved us through. We found the building where the animals were being housed and looked for Jane. She was just as frazzled and overwhelmed as when we spoke on the phone, but I could tell how relieved she was to see us. After putting us to work cleaning out cages and placing a frozen water bottle in each to bring the animals' body temperature down, Jane headed back out to go door to door in a boat, checking for stranded animals that would be brought back to the center.

We all have images in our minds of the flooding from Katrina, but what those images cannot show is how awful the air was. New Orleans was seeing temperatures of ninety to a hundred degrees, with 90 percent humidity. The sweltering heat was so hard for the animals to deal with. It ended up killing many of them.

People would come in looking for their pets, recounting horrific stories about what they themselves had done to survive. How they'd lost their parents or their spouses or their homes. Many had nothing left but the clothes they were wearing. For most of us, animals are family, and these folks were able to come back for their pets. I can tell you that when a reunification happened, there wasn't a dry eye in the house. It made every stressful minute worth it for us volunteers. But then there were the animals no one came for. Every day, with heavy hearts, we'd have to send some away, to any shelter anywhere in the country that would take them, to make room for the hundreds more being brought in.

Judie with rescued cats in New Orleans.

My background is in information technology. Whenever I'm confronted with a problem, I go into data-minded, solution-oriented mode. Watching all this unfold, I knew the only way to guarantee the best possible outcome for these families was to have a software program to track the animals.

As soon as I returned to my home in Laguna Beach, I teamed up with a database specialist and a few others to create a program for Jane's group, Animal Rescue New Orleans. Each animal would be logged as it came into the makeshift shelter and tracked if it was sent anywhere other than back to its family. We got the system up and running immediately. Over the next six months, I worked twelve hours a day to reunite as many pets as possible with their families. People continued to come back for their animals. We never gave up hope. I returned to New Orleans a few times in 2006 to train volunteers on using the system, and I provided support over the phone. It was the least I could do. It was also all I could do at the time. There were so many animals and so few resources to help them.

The whole time, I kept thinking that this tragedy within a tragedy was preventable. And that the same thing absolutely could happen in California. Officials in my state were closing their eyes and hoping the catastrophe wouldn't come on their watch. Properly preparing for disaster is a monumental task with countless moving parts. Doing it right takes resources and a willingness to be unpopular while the public gets educated about the cost of inaction. Not everyone will understand right away that investing to prevent a problem today can avoid untold damages and tragedy down the road.

In Louisiana, microchipping would have changed the outcome for many of the animals and their families. We'd eventually get a microchip bill done in California for shelter animals, though it would take more than a decade.

But in 2006, after my experience in New Orleans, I knew that in the near term, the most impactful thing I could do was to tackle California's dramatic pet overpopulation problem. Euthanasia rates in my state were already equivalent to four or five Katrina events every year. I couldn't imagine if you added a natural disaster on top of that. A spay and neuter law would do more to reduce the sheer number of animals in need of rescuing than anything else. No one was even talking about this solution, much less working toward it. I knew this was where my focus needed to be.

■ ■ ■

Los Angeles had agreed to take some sheltered animals from New Orleans. Ed Boks was General Manager of LA Animal Services (LAAS) at the time. He called a press conference to announce a Clear the Shelters event. The goal was to get as many animals as possible adopted or fostered out to make room for new arrivals from Louisiana.

Ed was determined to make lasting changes in the city and had the position to do it. During his tenure, adoptions rose and euthanasia rates dropped steadily. He understood that spay and neuter requirements work more than anything else. If you spend enough time in animal welfare, as he had, it becomes very clear that you can explain the benefits of sterilization to pet owners all day long. But even if they understand the need, unless it's mandatory, the majority won't do it. On the other hand, most will comply with a law.

I drove up to Los Angeles for the press conference and went to introduce myself to Ed afterward. I told him about everything I'd seen in New Orleans. Would he be interested in working together on spay and neuter legislation in California? He didn't hesitate. *Absolutely.*

We met in Ed's office the following week. I've always loved working with people who roll up their sleeves and swing into action when they have a good idea to translate into legislation. That was my experience with Ed from day one.

Going into that meeting, I had a laundry list of things we could do to help mitigate the overall pet overpopulation problem. At the top was spay and neuter, but I was also ready to get to work on systematic microchipping of all dogs and cats. A longer-term goal was to force pet stores to stop doing business with puppy mills and start offering shelter animals for adoption instead.

You could feel the excitement in the air in Ed's office. Spay and neuter ordinances had drastically reduced shelter populations in parts of California. Santa Cruz was a prime example, and we used it as a model. Turning that city's approach into a state law would accelerate the movement. Everyone would benefit—the animals, of course, and all of us who care about animal welfare. Taxpayers would come out way ahead too, reducing the massive spending that it takes to care for abandoned animals.

One of the people in the meeting was the head of LAAS field operations. He was fully on board with the bill idea but said there was a more pressing matter he hoped we could resolve first: that it was illegal for a humane officer to break into a vehicle if an animal inside was in imminent danger. I couldn't believe my ears. All those dogs I'd seen left in cars while their owners ran to do what was supposed to be a quick errand . . . A humane officer who saw the same thing wasn't allowed to break in to save the dogs, even if they were in extreme distress. There were documented instances of animal control staff watching helplessly as dogs tore up the inside of cars, fighting for breath, having brain seizures, dying before their eyes, while they waited for police officers who were out on higher priority calls.

There was a broad need to educate pet owners about this danger. The temperature in a car parked in the sun can jump to unbearable levels within minutes, even in mildly warm weather, even with the window cracked. Don't ever leave your dogs in your cars!

But in the meantime, this law urgently needed to change.

For the next year, we worked nonstop to bring lawmakers to our side. Ed and I traveled back and forth to Sacramento to advocate for the bill and testify at hearings. The city of LA sponsored the legislation and made its lobbyists available to provide support and join us in hearings. We explained what animal control officers were seeing in the field and the simple solution the bill offered. Humane officers would be authorized to handle these calls and then deal with all the follow-up, including keeping the animals safe while they tracked down the owners and ultimately issuing citations. A few people whined about their "property rights," referring mostly to their cars, but sometimes to their animals as well. We gave lawmakers every assurance that breaking into a car would always be the last resort and that a specific procedure would be followed in every instance. Humane officers would have a special thermometer to measure the temperature in the car. If it exceeded a certain threshold, they'd open the door using a Slim Jim tool—causing no damage. Once the animal was removed, they'd leave a ticket on the window and contact the owner.

It was a perfectly sensible law with no downside for anyone. One of those bills it's hard for legislators not to get behind. Many of the people I spoke with at the Capitol couldn't believe this was even an issue. Wait, animal control officers have to watch animals suffocate to death because they'd not allowed to force entry into cars? How can that be?

Senator Liz Figueroa, who I had met working on legislation to save heritage trees in California the year before, authored the bill with Assemblymember Lloyd Levine, a major animal rights champion who'd be instrumental in the founding of SCIL, as the main coauthor. Senate Bill 1806, Animals in Unattended Motor Vehicles, sailed through the Senate on a 31-to-3 vote, then passed the Assembly 58-to-5. Governor Arnold Schwarzenegger signed it into law in September 2006.

Effective January 1, 2007, animal control officers had another tool in their toolbox to save animal lives, and those who endangered the animals in the first place could face fines and even jail time.

What seems perfectly logical today represented, at the time, a revolutionary way to think about the treatment of animals. Until then, overt acts of abuse were against the law, but leaving an animal in a car in conditions that put its life in danger was not recognized as a form of cruelty. We fixed that. It was a major milestone for all of us who want to change how people think about and treat animals.

A decade later, in August 2016, Governor Jerry Brown signed into law Assembly Bill 797, the California Right to Rescue Act, which grants legal immunity to any Good Samaritan who breaks into a car to save an animal's life. Although we were not the sponsor of AB 797, we actively supported it, and our bill helped pave the way for this big win. We built further on these successes in 2022 with the SCIL-sponsored Safe Transportation of Dogs and Cats Act. It mandates that the health and wellbeing of animals be protected while they are being transported by animal control agencies, shelters, or rescue groups contracting with shelters.

They might seem like small advances. And you may think the concepts behind these laws are no-brainers. Of course there should be legislation to protect animals in vehicles! But they were not no-brainers at the time. We had to work hard to ensure these protections went into place.

This is how we save and protect animals—one law at a time. All these years later, animal control officers still go out of their way to thank me and say that our 2006 bill allowed them to save animals that otherwise would have died.

After this first success, I was thinking, *okay, I get it, I understand how lawmaking works.* Animals are dying in unattended cars because only police officers can break in? Well then, let's pass a law that allows animal control officers to do what's necessary to save the animals. Let's assign responsibilities in a more logical way and prevent animal suffering. Lawmakers from both sides of the aisle agree. The bill gets signed into law and boom—the problem is solved. Simple!

My logic-driven mind was excited. If we had the facts on our side and came in with a compelling case, surely legislators would get behind other sensible proposals we brought to them.

Wouldn't they?

■ ■ ■

It was with this mindset that I prepared to start on the list I had brought to Ed's office at LA Animal Services the previous year. The close-knit team that had passed the dogs in hot cars bill, with a few other key stakeholders joining us, got to work drafting a spay and neuter bill, which became the California Healthy Pets Act, Assembly Bill 1634. Authored by Assemblymember Lloyd Levine, AB 1634 would require that all dogs and cats in California be spayed or neutered by the age of six months, with some exceptions.

The bill was introduced before the February deadline. We were expecting to see more opposition than with SB 1806 but nothing extreme. The facts were on our side. Laws like the one we were sponsoring produced results. We had proof. A spay and neuter ordinance in Santa Cruz had led to an estimated 56 percent decrease in the number of sheltered dogs and 60 percent for cats. Those kinds of numbers speak for themselves. Exemptions would be made for show dogs, service dogs, and other categories, and we could carve out more.

Responsible breeders got behind us quickly. They knew it was better for animals, for people, and for taxpayers if there were rules and reporting requirements that applied to everyone. As it stood, there was no penalty for backyard breeding operations that dumped litter after litter onto city streets and into county shelters. AB 1634 added a reasonable amount of regulation that would put a serious dent in the pet overpopulation problem. And we all knew there was a problem, right? You can't kill half a million pets a year in shelters and say there's no crisis, can you?

Turns out, some can.

Media coverage of the spay and neuter fight was off the charts. I worked hard to give the animals the best possible representation.

Starting in March, a month after the bill was introduced in the Assembly, and for the next sixteen months until it died on the Senate floor, the California Healthy Pets Act would generate levels of support and opposition the likes of which Sacramento had never seen. Both sides came to refer to it simply as "The Bill." Every hearing was packed to capacity with activists from both sides, with more waiting outside. We shut down entire floors of the Capitol. Media coverage was off the charts. I was invited to talk about the bill on local outlets as well as some national ones, including CNN and Fox

News. We even got international coverage on the BBC and in the Nikkei.

With these unprecedented levels of publicity and attention, people were telling me I had to step up my game to be the best possible voice for the animals. Until then, I had been working behind the scenes as a member of the animal protection community and speaking in front of big groups as a manager in my information technology career, but never on camera. Now I was called upon to be the face of something much bigger, to go out in front and lead the charge for the animals.

So I got some media training from friends who were in show business or PR professionals. I learned how to speak and conduct myself during hearings and when interacting with lawmakers. I learned how to present to the camera. Suddenly, I found myself writing press releases to document our progress and let people know what we needed them to do next. This was a whole new skill set I had to develop on the fly.

■ ■ ■

Support for AB 1634 was overwhelming. Elected officials from across the state were on our side. Law enforcement and animal services agencies backed us. Veterinarians too. Tens of thousands of individuals wrote to their legislators asking them to support the bill. This was before groups had long email lists and could drum up support just by blasting out a request. These letters were from individuals who heard about the bill through one channel or another and took the time to write to their representatives to tell them why they should vote yes.

While we were winning people over to our side by sharing facts and telling the truth about what was happening in rescues and shelters, those who use dogs to make money were spreading lies to kill the bill.

Brand-new groups were springing up out of nowhere to oppose us. They'd form new alliances and shape-shift constantly. Listening to the noise, you'd think there were as many people against the bill as there were for it. Nothing was further from the truth. The numbers were on our side—it wasn't even close.

As I watched this endless stream of people file into the Capitol to speak against the bill or stand out on the steps to gin up opposition, I couldn't stop wondering where they all were coming from. I'd been involved with animal rights for years, and I'd never seen or heard of any of them. Plus, they were all parroting the exact same talking points, like robots. Where were they getting them?

We were a massive grassroots movement, but they were creating the illusion that there was an equally large movement against us.

If you follow politics at all, you've probably heard the term opposition research. There's a whole industry out there of professionals who specialize in digging up dirt for political campaigns. Or, as in my case, if you're fighting for good legislation and you've got bad actors coming out of the woodwork to defeat it, you can bring in these experts to find out exactly who your opponents are, or who they are working for. After observing these carefully orchestrated attacks from the other side, I used some of the money we'd raised to hire big-name researchers. Folks who had worked on presidential campaigns and knew how to look under every rock and behind every door. You can't fight an enemy you don't know.

A few weeks later, I was presented with a 110-page opposition research report. It described in detail how a vast network of special interests had been set up to kill our bill. None of those individuals or groups I watched file into the Capitol were acting alone. Or spontaneously. All their words and moves were carefully coordinated. Strategically managed. It's called astroturfing—making the actions of a small special interest group appear to have grassroots support. No one in Sacramento had seen this kind of astroturfing before.

Lobbyists for the other side would spin the data to create a false narrative about the supposed downsides of spay and neuter laws (there aren't any). Expensive lobbyists do this better than anyone. And the lobbyists for the other side were top dollar.

It seemed like every group that made money off animals or the status quo had its name on the list. Breeders. People who bought from breeders. Groups that issued registration certificates to breeders. Stores selling dogs from breeders. Hunters. Groups selling guns to hunters. It was a "who's who" of animal exploiters and special interests, all determined to keep the bill from getting signed into law.

No wonder so many lawmakers were running scared.

CHAPTER 2

THE BIG BUSINESS OF ANIMAL CRUELTY

The Cattlemen's Association got in on the action right away, and I wondered why. As it was explained to me, some ranchers breed dogs on their farms as a side business. Since many of these dogs are sold as hunting dogs, the National Rifle Association got involved too.

The Hunte Corporation, the biggest puppy mill operator in the country, had a business model to protect. And it wasn't alone.

The more I heard about the operations of unscrupulous puppy mills, the more disgusted I was. In some facilities, undercover animal rights activists had found a thousand dogs crammed in together, living out miserable lives in miniscule, all-concrete spaces. Females were reported to spend their whole lives in nonstop confinement, with barely any food or water. Males were brought in to keep them pregnant every cycle. It still goes on today. These poor dogs produce litter after litter until they are "bred out," meaning they are physically incapable of producing more puppies. Then they get euthanized. If they are lucky. Oftentimes the operators just drown them or dump them into a pit and shoot them.

Misery and death aren't the cost of doing business for these mills. They *are* the business. Our bill was going to turn the spotlight on the despicable practices of the whole industry. And it was a direct threat to breeders operating in California. They wouldn't be able to keep breeding dogs until they died if they were spayed at six months old.

One of the most active opponents by far was the American Kennel Club (AKC). Some people associate the AKC brand with animal protection or pet merchandise, but its main business is issuing dog registration certificates, and puppy mills pay big money for those papers. Anything that could interfere with mill operations was therefore perceived as a threat. AKC top executives had given themselves fat raises a few years before, creating even more incentives to keep a good thing going. The tax filing included in the opposition research report showed that in 2007, when our bill was introduced, the AKC president's pay had just been increased to over $500,000 a year. The other top brass was making between a quarter and a half a million annually.

We could assume that, if the breeding business stopped booming, all those paychecks would be at risk.

A few years earlier, in response to bad press about its collaboration with puppy mills, the AKC had set up a "High Volume Breeders" committee. Has a nicer ring to it than puppy mill committee, doesn't it? This new committee was headed by AKC board member Patti Strand, herself a breeder and AKC judge. Strand was also head of NAIA and NAIA Trust, two other organizations masquerading as animal welfare groups that were spearheading the attacks on the spay and neuter bill. NAIA stands for National Animal Interest Alliance, but its mission is to protect the interests of animal *owners.*

According to the opposition research, NAIA was the nexus of all these different animal exploiters fighting AB 1634, and it was coordinating their lobbying efforts.

Strand and her husband had cowritten a book describing how those of us who care about animal welfare had hijacked the humane movement. A defender of fur farm breeding, she maintained that animals are the property of the people who own them, and that any laws restricting what they can do with those animals infringe on their property rights.

This is literally the opposite of how animal rights advocates see the world.

So the AKC committee appeared to be coordinating with the Hunte Corporation, and all these different groups were working with major pet store chains that purchased dogs from puppy mills. Chief among them was Petland, which had 120 stores across the country at the time and was planning to open twenty-five more. You can bet it was doing whatever it could to ensure a steady supply of dogs to fill its cages and line its pockets.

This is what we were dealing with. People who were making a fortune off dogs. Benefiting from the status quo. Determined to keep their good thing going, no matter how many animals wound up being mistreated by breeders and dying in shelters.

■ ■ ■

New groups were constantly being formed for the sole purpose of defeating our bill. One was a political action committee called

PetPAC. It was set up and run by Bill Hemby, a longtime lobbyist for the California Organization of Police and Sheriffs (a.k.a. COPS) and himself a dog breeder. Through PetPAC, he started raising massive amounts of money to defeat AB 1634 and promising to fund primary challengers for any legislator who voted for it. Hemby would stand out on the steps of the Capitol and hand out PetPAC lapel pins to anyone who would wear one. No one had ever seen guerrilla marketing like this in Sacramento. Everywhere people went, he and the opposition were there.

Not surprisingly, the lobbyists the other side hired to pressure lawmakers directly were themselves the Wild West, anything goes types. Many were from the same firm that had spent years helping big tobacco make the case that smoking is actually good for you. Now they were using that same kind of spin doctoring to produce a steady stream of misinformation and disinformation about the spay and neuter bill.

We'd do actual research and present real data to show precisely how pet overpopulation was impacting animals, veterinarians, rescue groups, shelter professionals, and taxpayers, and how AB 1634 would reduce that impact. Everything was documented, including with dozens of hours of video. Our opponents would waltz in with glossy brochures and dazzling charts full of made-up numbers, along with pictures of dogs living their best lives in puppy factories and pet stores. It all looked so professional, so polished. So believable. But none of it was real. Almost every statement and statistic was pure fabrication. You'll never see a photo of a real dog in a real puppy mill because conditions are too miserable to show. None of that mattered during this fight. The lawmakers listening were being presented with an alternative narrative. It may have been all fake, but it would give them cover if they opted to vote against our bill. Giving them that cover was the goal.

Hemby and his lobbyists were ruthless and relentless with their disinformation campaign. They handed out flyers and posters referring to AB 1634 as the "Pet Extinction Act," and got that name to stick. On television, Hemby declared that our bill was designed to "eliminate all dogs and cats in California." Uninformed observers became convinced that there would be no more police dogs, guide dogs, or search and rescue dogs in the state, ever again. Definitely no purebreds. Probably no dogs and cats at all. They'd heard it so often, it must be true, right?

All this spin and fearmongering got into people's heads.

This was my introduction to one of the saddest truths about our political system: it is possible, and even easy, for deep-pocketed special interests to sow so much fear and confusion over a bill that it has almost no chance of passing. Newspapers were running articles about how the issue was "dividing pet lovers." As if the people fighting to keep making money off animals cared about them as much as those of us working to reduce euthanasia rates!

Depressingly, much of the media bought into it. Astroturf groups with names like "Veterinarians Against AB 1634" would crop up out of nowhere and get tons of press coverage. The opinion pages were another powerful vehicle for scaremongering. Letters to the editor were being submitted by people from every breed club in the state saying that intake and euthanasia rates were declining, when actually they were going through the roof. A group calling itself "We the People for Pets" handed out a booklet that included a cartoon portraying me as a witch, standing in the middle of the "Animal Rights Politicians' Graveyard." It showed the caricature of me amidst headstones with the names of pro-animal legislators, surrounded by plots reserved for other politicians I was working with. PETA president Ingrid Newkirk and Wayne Pacelle, then-president of the Humane

Society of the United States (HSUS), the usual targets of these exploiters, got dragged into the propaganda materials as well. Another group portrayed us as Brown Shirts going door to door, inspecting animals to make sure none were intact.

The opposition's messaging was all about freedom, property rights, and privacy. Every one of their "testimonials" concluded the same way: if the spay and neuter law passed, within a generation, there might not be any more cats or dogs in California.

Even with the truth on your side, it's virtually impossible to compete with this kind of coordinated disinformation campaign backed by unlimited resources.

I had never worked so hard in my life. Every day, I arrived when the Capitol opened and stayed until it closed. Up and down the stairs I ran, dashing into legislators' offices, educating their staff, going over the details of the bill one more time, explaining again exactly what it would and wouldn't do, begging them to do the right thing.

One lawmaker heard me out as I told her about the tragedy unfolding in California shelters and the role overbreeding was playing in it. Not knowing how much time I had in the meeting, I really dumbed down my presentation so a first grader could get the gist. She listened so intently, I was sure I'd gotten another yes vote. Until she pushed her chair back from the table and said, "My dog is the best dog in the world. I would never want a puppy from another dog." Had she heard anything I'd said? Did she realize that if every dog owner who thinks their dog is the best in the world (that's all of us) kept breeding their pet, the overpopulation crisis would keep getting worse? Yes, she explained, she understood all that, but her dog was *truly* the best.

That was just too much for me. I was so dumbfounded that I turned to my lobbyist and asked him to finish the meeting while I waited in the hallway. He came out a few minutes later, chuckling and shaking his head. Thankfully, he had me covered.

■ ■ ■

AB 1634 was introduced on February 26, 2007.

It was referred to its first committee, Assembly Business and Professions, a month later, and only made it out at the end of April. Next stop: re-referral to the Appropriations Committee, where it sat for another month.

Appropriations is where lawmakers determine the fiscal impact a bill will have if it becomes law, and who will bear the related cost. Countless bills never make it out of that committee. All the data was on our side when it came to saving taxpayers money. But lawmakers were listening to the other side's scare tactics too, and sometimes that was all they heard.

The special interests were working overtime to get lawmakers to lay off the vote—that's code for don't vote at all. When you see NVR next to a legislator's name, it stands for "no vote recorded." Usually it means they were sitting at their desk when the vote was taken but didn't have the spine to push the yes or no button. It's an easy way out that the people California voters send to Sacramento take advantage of too often. And boy, did they use it with AB 1634.

We squeaked out of Appropriations mid-May after several re-referrals, and the bill finally went to a floor vote on May 31. There are eighty assemblymembers, so we needed at least forty-one ayes to move the bill out of that chamber and into the State Senate.

Final tally: ayes thirty-seven, noes thirty, NVR thirteen.

We asked for reconsideration, which you can only do once, and it was granted. The bill was coming back one more time. We worked the votes, lobbied like crazy, worked the votes some more . . . and on June 6, we *finally* got over the threshold. Exactly forty-one ayes. None to spare. We had to beg and grovel for every vote, pull out every stop. In some cases, that involved recruiting famous or influential constituents to arrange meetings with their representatives and urge them to vote yes. When lawmakers were willing, we'd organize private tours of shelters in their districts so they could see for themselves how many animals were suffering and dying. There's nothing like giving legislators an up-close view of the problem they're being asked to solve. Those visits and tours brought the last few members over to our side.

There was only one NVR left as lawmakers were forced to get off the fence. Thirty-eight still voted no.

One of them was a Republican from Orange County, representing a district near where I live. He had actually spoken on the floor in favor of the bill, enthusiastically, and supported it up until the last day, when he flipped.

The day after the vote, I saw him at the Sacramento airport, which is small, so it's hard to hide from someone you don't want to see. We were on the same flight back to Orange County.

I got in the boarding line behind him and asked, "What happened? You spoke on the floor in favor of our bill. You sounded like you meant it. Then you voted against it. Why did you flip?"

"Well," he said, "I read the bill, I understood what you were trying to do with it, and I agreed that it was a good idea. So I voted for it. Then my phone started ringing off the hook. My party was telling me I needed to fall off, or else."

"So you told everyone you supported the bill. Your conscience told you to vote yes right up until the last day. Then your party told you to vote no, and you listened to your party?"

"That's correct."

It took me a minute to absorb this. Finally, I said, "You know, listening to you speak on the floor, I had hope that you'd do the right thing. And that you'd help pull other Republicans over to our side."

"Don't hold your breath, Judie. They told me they'd break my kneecaps if I voted for it."

Normally, the bill should have started the next leg of its journey in the Senate Local Government Committee later in June, but the chair made it clear she didn't want anything to do with it. Another sad reality of Sacramento: if a committee chair doesn't like a bill, they can simply fail to bring it up for a vote, which can effectively kill it.

As I would later find out, this particular committee chair's chief of staff was a dog breeder, and the pressure was coming from him. It was totally by chance that this came to light. An Assembly staffer assigned to help pass our bill noticed a tear-off flyer on the bulletin board in the garage of the Capitol building advertising labradoodles for sale. On a hunch, the staffer called the number, and the chair's chief of staff answered. Connection made.

An ethics complaint was then filed. Not by me—I only heard about all this once the session was over. Next thing we knew, AB 1634 had miraculously made it through that committee.

Like so many things, passing legislation takes a village, and then some.

■ ■ ■

On July 11, the day the bill was supposed to come up for its first vote in a Senate committee, I was invited on CNN's *American Morning with Kiran Chetry* for an on-air debate with Kelley Moran, the state campaign director for PetPAC.

Bob Barker and me in Chicago with Paula Fasseas and Alderman Ed Burke, who sponsored the spay and neuter ordinance.

Early morning on CNN meant about 4:00 a.m. in my time zone. My hair was still wet from the shower, and I had just taken my first sip of coffee when the episode kicked off with a video of Bob Barker, a true animal lover and huge proponent of spay and neuter. He was retiring that year from three and a half decades as the host of *The Price is Right* and was using his platform to help pass our bill. Every information packet we had dropped off at the offices of elected officials included a letter from Bob, urging them to "Come on down . . . to help the animals." Bob was such a great ally of ours in every battle, every step of the way. I'd met him through a friend at one of the LA shelters when AB 1634 was first being introduced. Right away, he started doing everything he could to help, including attending our kickoff press conference and speaking to the LA City Council about the ordinance I was simultaneously helping pass there. He even came to Chicago with me to speak to the city council and meet with the members about spay and neuter ordinances.

I'd watch him race up and down the stairs, dash into offices and meetings insisting that we keep going, and think, this man has more energy than anyone I knew—even in his mid-80s!

In the video that started the CNN segment, Bob laid out the problem for the audience: too many dogs and cats being born means too many dogs and cats being killed. Simple as that. His clip was followed by one of Jon Provost, the actor who played Timmy Martin on seven seasons of the TV show *Lassie*. He was working for the other side, with the wild claim that people had been breeding collies for decades to get Lassie's specific look. All this work would be lost if our bill passed.

So on one side, we had Bob Barker telling people that with all the taxpayer dollars that would be saved, the price is right for this legislation. On the other, you had Timmy Martin saying Lassie would never come home if AB 1634 passed.

Hollywood getting involved did wonders for drawing national attention to the issue.

As soon as we were live, Moran from PetPAC jumped right in, spinning as fast as he could to squeeze in every talking point and mistruth the opposition had used against us. He claimed everyone who opposed the bill was simply a California pet owner (they were mostly dog breeders). According to him, the bill would lead to the extinction of all dogs and cats in our state, even wiping out the

Bob testifying in Chicago.

Bob Barker attended and spoke at multiple press conferences in Los Angeles and Sacramento as a champion of AB 1634.

Lassie family. This was his way of putting fear into the audience's hearts and pulling at their heartstrings at the same time. He had a collie posted outside the Capitol starting at 8:00 a.m. that day to drive the point home. As Moran told it, there would be no more police canines or service dogs in our state ever again if this legislation passed.

I did my best to explain that AB 1634 was not a breeding ban and that Lassie would be safe. Instead, the bill was an example of what legislation is supposed to do: compel people to do the right thing when education outreach and voluntary programs have failed. The pet overpopulation was bad and getting worse because people were not getting their companion animals sterilized.

After falsely claiming that the California Veterinary Medical Board and all police associations opposed the bill, Moran went at AB 1634 from a money angle, suggesting that city and county budgets would skyrocket if they had to enforce a spay and neuter law. We had irrefutable proof that costs would never match what governments were paying to have shelters take in, care for, and euthanize hundreds and thousands of dogs and cats every year, but it didn't matter to him.

Moran kept trying to direct viewers to his website, and I kept telling them if they wanted accurate information, they should go to the website my then-husband and I had set up to debunk their lies one by one. We called it petpacnonsense. When you're trying to fight lies with truth, rebuttal websites are a great resource.

At the end of the segment, Moran said he'd see us at 8:00 a.m. when the Capitol opened and promised that his side would kill the bill that day.

■ ■ ■

The bill didn't die that day, but our opponents got the next best outcome: AB 1634 was stalled for a year by the chair of the Senate Local Government Committee. I knew we were in trouble when I saw that the opposition's propaganda pamphlet included a photo of the chair with a Lassie look-alike in her office. As chair, she had the power to refuse to bring a bill up for a vote, and that's what she did here. No way would the committee members "roll the chair," as it's referred to when members vote yes on a bill that the chair is not supporting.

We needed time to win her over.

For the next twelve months, we worked nonstop to educate the chair and other lawmakers. We explained and reexplained all the upsides of the bill. Addressed every one of their concerns. Tried to counter the firehose of falsehoods from the other side. Hoped against hope that these senators would set aside their petty disputes and party pressures and do the right thing. I went from one office to the next, thoughts racing through my mind, including wondering if I was going to spend the rest of my life running up and down those stairs.

It took us over a year, but we finally got the bill out of the Senate Local Government Committee, and in the summer of 2008, it finally came up for a floor vote. By that time, it had a new name, and had been watered down so much that it was in many ways unrecognizable. It was still alive, but barely. On the morning of the vote, a senator who had promised to support us ran up to me in the rotunda and pulled me aside. She warned me to make sure the bill didn't get brought to the floor. The Women's Caucus had met earlier that morning, and the chair told the others they needed to vote no. The senator issuing that order was termed out, meaning she was ineligible to run again, and Lloyd Levine, the author of the bill, was running for her seat. Problem was, so was one of the senator's close friends. Clearly, a high-profile success right before the election would give Assemblymember Levine, a well-regarded advocate for animal rights, a huge advantage over her best buddy.

Translation: after doing battle for over a year against what seemed like every animal-exploiting special interest in the country, the final nail in the coffin of AB 1634 was about to be hammered in by a politician whose top priority was to hand her seat off to her friend.

State Senator Alex Padilla (now the senior US Senator for California) was acting as floor manager for the bill. I tracked him down and told him what was happening. I begged him not to call for the vote. He said he had no choice. Only the author could request a cancellation.

We wanted everybody to know what the legislature was voting on and that there was only one right way to vote.

I ran to find Assemblymember Levine. He was chairing a committee meeting and there was no way for me to get word to him of what was taking place on the other side of the building. Our bill was being voted on, and I wasn't sure if the author even knew it was happening.

Feeling more alone than ever and with a pit in my stomach, I dashed up the stairs to watch from the balcony as State Senator Padilla called the vote: "Here it is," he began, "the bill you've all been waiting for."

The time and effort and personal commitment that went into getting AB 1634 to that point started long before it reached the Senate floor. People had been working on the issue for decades, dedicated their lives to it. I'd visited shelters up and down the state. Staffers and vets couldn't do enough to express their gratitude. They were so hopeful that the gut-wrenching and totally avoidable tragedy they experienced day after day would end. Some of these shelters were bringing in over 50,000 animals a year and killing two-thirds of them. The emotional toll it was taking on employees and volunteers was unfathomable.

Sometimes I'd pull into the parking lot at a shelter and staffers would come rushing out to say, "We've been waiting for you!" I knew what they meant. They were waiting for a solution, for some relief from the unbearable, unnecessary pain they were experiencing.

Their sentiment that nobody cared was justified. Year after year, California's budget for shelters was getting smaller, leaving them with fewer resources to deal with more animals. Nothing was being done at the state level to address overbreeding and overpopulation. Our bill was their hope. By calling attention to the tragedy unfolding day after day in the shelters, it had created a movement, and they were part of it.

By the time the Senate vote took place, we had received almost 30,000 letters of support. The list of organizations and cities that backed us was fifteen full pages long. Supporters had packed into the building for every hearing. History was being made. We could feel it.

Until that day.

My heart sank as I watched the floor session begin. Senators were making dog puns and cracking jokes while explaining why they would be voting no. I knew the bill was not going to pass. At gavel down, after an excruciatingly long day, we only had five ayes. Twenty-seven voted against the bill. Eight couldn't be bothered to take a position at all.

Technically, we could bring the bill back for another vote later, but we knew the outcome would be the same. It was over.

Now, I've been through some tough times in my life, and it takes a lot for me to break down in tears. But when the reality of that vote sank in, I couldn't hold back. Locked inside a stall in one of the bathrooms on the fourth floor, I cried my eyes out. All those people who had poured their hearts and souls into the bill were counting on me to get it passed. We'd mobilized so many supporters, raised so much money, gotten so many people's hopes up, and come so close to defeating all those special interests—only to have it all torn away because of petty rivalries and cowardly politicians. It was truly painful. Soul-crushing. Infuriating.

■ ■ ■

As I was packing up the small apartment I'd rented near the Capitol to head home to Laguna Beach, my phone rang. It was *LA Times* reporter Carla Hall. A real animal lover, Carla had been following the bill closely, and had contacted me many times for stories about it.

"Oh, Judie, what happened?"

"Honestly, Carla, the bill could have said the sky is blue and the ocean is deep, and they would have voted against it."

I stand by that statement.

By the time it died, AB 1634 had been put on hold for a whole year, amended eleven times, and diluted by gigantic exemptions and loopholes. It had been renamed the California Responsible Pet Owners Act to give it a new look and reflect its much narrower scope. We had addressed every single concern raised by our opponents. In its final form, pets only had to be sterilized if they were found, more than once, to be unlicensed, running loose, or impounded. It was so watered down that even the AKC changed its position to neutral. None of that mattered. A few legislators were focused only on their own political careers and those of their friends. Not for the first or the last time, the poor suffering shelter animals were the losers.

Carla's article about the AB 1634 battle, "The Political Education of Judie Mancuso," ran in the *LA Times* on August 31, 2008. She couldn't have found a more perfect title.

My main mentor during that period was Assemblymember Lloyd Levine. Early in 2007, as we watched the tentacles of special interests tighten around the bill, he took me aside and explained how things worked. That I'd never get anywhere in Sacramento if people thought I was a one-woman show and a one-hit wonder. To get this bill and others across the finish line, I'd need an ongoing presence in the Capitol and an official structure behind me. Success would require hiring top lobbyists and creating my own organization to rally like-minded individuals and groups.

In sum, I needed to go big or go home.

Challenge accepted.

■ ■ ■

One of the first people I contacted was Haze Lynn. Haze had reached out to me early in 2007, right after the spay and neuter bill was introduced, to ask how she could help, and quickly became one of my strongest allies. We were in constant contact throughout the year. Since I had been living in Laguna Beach for more than a decade by that time, I didn't have connections with the rescue community in Los Angeles. Haze knew them all.

Before long, I was being introduced to the people I needed to know to get the nonprofit up and running. A wealthy animal lover offered to host a meet and greet in the theater of her Beverly Hills mansion. After she introduced me to the crowd, I explained what I was trying to accomplish with the spay and neuter bill, and how I intended to bring animal rights into the heart of the conversation in the legislature through the new nonprofit. As soon as I'd finished, a man I'd never met held his wallet up in the air. From it, he withdrew a check folded into a tiny rectangle. As if performing a magic trick, he carefully unfolded the check and showed the crowd that it was blank. It was all quite dramatic and exciting. Then he filled in the amount: $20,000. I'd never dreamed of raising that much all at once. Until then, we'd been scraping money together just to get by and begging for every penny of it.

He asked who to write the check to.

I'd put a lot of thought into finding the right name for my new group. It had to reflect exactly what I was setting out to accomplish. Something like "Pets and Paws" could work, but it wasn't big enough. What if we wanted to do a bill on marine life? (In 2021, we cosponsored the Whale Entanglement Prevention Act with the Center for Biological Diversity. It didn't pass, but that doesn't mean we won't succeed next time.) Or one focused on plant-based eating to save farm animals and the planet? (We sponsored legislation in 2018 that ensures plant-based options are available in all state healthcare facilities and prisons, and the SCIL-sponsored Child Nutrition Act of 2022 incentivizes K–12 schools in California to serve plant-based meals and beverages.)

Even back in 2007, I knew the name needed to reflect a broad vision that could encompass every kind of effort to save and protect animals, and the planet too, since it's all interrelated. Why save the animals if there's nowhere for them to live?

When it came down to it, in my heart of hearts, my goal was to spread compassion. In legislatures, yes, but also throughout society. Too many people live their lives without giving a second thought to the impacts of their actions on animals or their fellow humans, on our habitats and ecosystems. I wanted to change that. Through education. Through advocacy. Through new laws.

More compassion was the key to a better future for animals and people.

After days of brainstorming and online research, I came up with "Social Compassion." The two words were not used together anywhere at the time. I registered Social Compassion as a 501(c)(3) with the Secretary of State in July 2007. "Social Compassion in Legislation" as a 501(c)(4) was created at the same time as the vehicle for lobbying work. One of the big selling points for me was the acronym SCIL (pronounced like "skill"). I knew it would take a lot of skill for us to be successful.

These names felt big enough. They felt right.

So when I got the question at this big fundraising event, I responded with pride in my voice: "You can make the check out to Social Compassion in Legislation. And thank you!"

Holding up the check was attorney Steven Bernheim, a man who has made it his life's mission to use his resources to ease animal and human suffering through direct action. Steven is a pillar who has kept the nonprofit up and running from day one, including by coming through with a massive contribution late in 2020, when COVID-19 had caused our fundraising to grind to a halt.

That evening put me on a course I could never have imagined. It was also there that I first met Dr. Gary Michelson. An orthopedic spinal surgeon, inventor, and philanthropist, Dr. Michelson has a deeper commitment to helping people and pets than anyone I know. And believe me, over the years I've gotten to know a lot of people who do a lot of good! Meeting him that day, and benefiting from his continued support ever since, has been life-changing for me and SCIL.

It seemed everyone I talked to during the AB 1634 saga told me I absolutely should speak to Paula Kent Meehan and Erika Brunson. In doing my research before meeting them, I discovered two incredibly successful businesspeople and philanthropists who were good friends and partners in a quest to reduce pet overpopulation in California. Paula cofounded and ran the Redken haircare brand.

Our first fundraiser brought together more political power than I could have hoped. Pictured from left to right, with their titles at the time, are Assemblymember Mike Gatto, West Hollywood City Councilmember John D'Amico, Los Angeles City Councilmember Paul Koretz, Assemblymember Kevin de León, Assemblymember Pedro Nava, me, Assemblymember Ted Lieu, Los Angeles City Councilmember Tony Cardenas, and Assemblymember Jose Solorio.

Erika had a successful career as a furniture maker and interior designer. What an inspiration to see such powerful women using their time and treasure to make a meaningful difference in the lives of animals.

Anxious to see my new nonprofit get off to a strong start, Ed Boks set up a meeting with Paula and Erika in his office at the LAAS headquarters in downtown Los Angeles. Naturally, the prospect of having a new animal rights organization take the fight to Sacramento appealed to them. So much so that each wrote me a $10,000 check right there on the spot.

Paula then offered to host a launch party at her Beverly Hills home. Little did I know then that she lived in the former estate of

Elvis Presley! She hosted us in her Japanese tea garden and helped us fill it with friends old and new, including Bob Barker, Debbie Reynolds, Bijan, Cesar Millan, and several members of the LA City Council and state legislature.

Up until the day of their deaths, Paula in 2014 and Erika in 2022, they did everything they could to help SCIL and all the animals.

At that first party, Bob Barker pitched the crowd, then kicked off the donations with a pledge. Next thing I knew, Dr. Michelson was offering $25,000 and looking for a match. Erika and Margie Perenchio both met the challenge. Margie was a longtime friend of Erika's and fellow socialite. She was as excited as anyone to get behind the new nonprofit, financially and in countless other ways. She would stay involved with and supportive of us through the early 2020s, including by serving on the board for several years.

SCIL's launch was beyond anything I had dared hope for. Suddenly, I had serious financial backing and a team of supporters who were as committed to the cause as I was.

One thing I'd understood at a deep level is that it takes all kinds of help to get things done in Sacramento, but you can't get anywhere without money to hire the professionals needed.

The next thing we'd need was people. Thankfully, I wasn't starting from scratch. Incredible allies had emerged during the AB 1634 fight, courageous animal lovers who had no fears about putting principles above politics and standing up to special interests. Friends I'd been doing animal rights work with for years, people whose values were totally aligned with mine, were quick to come aboard. Soon, we had created our own army.

SCIL's motto is "Saving and Protecting Animals One Law at a Time." The spay and neuter bill was ground zero for the movement we started. SCIL was the vehicle through which it would continue.

CHAPTER 3

WELCOME TO SACRAMENTO, WHERE EVEN THE SIMPLEST THINGS ARE COMPLICATED

When I ran for California State Assembly in 2022, voters often asked about my qualifications. Well, I'd say, the nonprofit I founded in 2007, and have been running ever since, has sponsored over sixty bills and had twenty-two signed into law (the totals are higher now).

Anyone who had even a passing familiarity with the legislative process understood how big these numbers were and was rightfully impressed. Others who did not know the slog of legislating were skeptical. *Only twenty-two laws in fifteen years? What is that, one and a half a year?*

On the campaign trail, you usually only have a few minutes to win people over. There's not enough time to explain to the uninitiated how hard it is to get things done in Sacramento. How sometimes you have to bring the same bill back several times to get it passed. For instance, anyone who has studied pet overpopulation knows that microchipping shelter animals makes a huge difference and should be mandatory. In 2011, State Senator Ted Lieu, now a US Representative, introduced a SCIL-sponsored bill to that effect. The bill made it through both houses. Governor Jerry Brown vetoed it.

State Senator Ling Ling Chang authored another iteration called the Pet Microchipping Bill in 2019. It too sailed through both chambers only to be vetoed by Governor Gavin Newsom. We finally got it signed into law in 2020, after addressing the governor's concerns, nine years after the first version was introduced! Our bill to modernize pet blood banks in California—a straightforward, commonsense, money-saving law—took three whole years to get passed.

Bringing the same bill back a second or third time involves just as many hours of work and resources as the first attempt. The whole process essentially starts over. People don't realize how time- and labor-intensive this work is. I certainly didn't when I started SCIL.

There's never a straight line from a bill being introduced to it being signed into law. Roadblocks pop up at every turn. Usually, each bill goes through at least two committees in each house, one policy committee and a fiscal committee called appropriations, to determine what part of the code will need to be changed and where the costs will fall. Bills can easily die in any one of those committees.

Don't get me wrong, not all ideas are good. Triage is normal. But a bill can get axed because a committee chair doesn't like it or doesn't want to deal with the issue it addresses. In such cases, the chair simply fails to bring it up for a vote. "No time, we've got other, more pressing priorities." That's all the justification they need.

A lawmaker who really has it in for you or your bill can make sure it gets sent to three different committees, maximizing the chances of it getting killed somewhere along the line. This has happened to us more than once. "Triple referrals" are usually a death knell. They send a clear message that someone in leadership has an agenda or a fear related to your bill but is too weak to say it to your face.

A bill that makes it out of committees might get shot down in one of the two house floor votes. Remember that AB 1634, the spay and neuter bill, passed the Assembly after thousands of hours of lobbying and volunteer efforts, only to get torpedoed on the Senate floor.

The next leg of the journey is just as dangerous for a bill that makes it through all the committees and both chambers because it then goes to the governor's desk, where the veto pen awaits. Every governor has an army of staffers poring over texts and trying to weed out as many as possible, especially ones that involve costs that won't be offset or covered through any kind of funding mechanism. It takes a two-thirds vote in each house to override a veto. The last time that happened was in 1980. Basically, if the governor says no, it's the end of the road for that year.

During his seven years in office, Governor Schwarzenegger shot down more than a quarter of the bills that came before him after passing both houses. One year, he vetoed over 35 percent.

Democratic governors also use their veto power, of course. In 2019, it was Governor Newsom who vetoed an earlier version of our Blood Bank Modernization Act before signing a third iteration into law in 2021. In 2018, Governor Brown took his veto pen to Senate Bill 1487, our Iconic African Species Protection Act, which would have made it illegal to possess body parts from eleven endangered species including African elephants, lions, leopards, black or white rhinos, and giraffes. Symbolically, the timing could not have been more painful, since that was the year we said goodbye to Sudan, the world's last male northern white rhino. The Trump Administration was rolling back federal protections for all these animals. Despite the concessions we made and the assurances we gave, Governor Brown threw out the bill, claiming it would be unenforceable. It wasn't true. The author had gone to great lengths to address enforcement concerns. We had crafted the bill in consultation with the legal departments of internationally renowned organizations to ensure it could survive inevitable court challenges. But the governor had the last word. After years of hard work by us and other animal protection groups on a bill to save these majestic species, the stroke of a pen sent us back to the drawing board.

We brought it back in 2020 with Senate Bill 1175, again authored by State Senator Henry Stern. This time, the opposition focused mostly on bogus evidence that trophy hunting contributes to the conservation of species in Africa. SB 1175 died in committee.

Brendan Cummings, Katie Cleary, Senator Henry Stern, Nick Sackett, and me holding a press conference for the Iconic African Species Act in 2018.

Hundreds of hours of work went into each of these failed efforts.

As I write, we've had nine bills die on the governor's desk. Some have since been passed after being reintroduced in other forms, under other names, including our blood banks and microchipping bills. Others remain in the pipeline. The Deforestation-Free Procurement Act, cosponsored by SCIL and Friends of the Earth, would mandate that the state of California only contract with companies that have proven sustainable practices for the procurement of products harvested from tropical forests. First introduced by Assemblymember Ash Kalra in 2019, the bill died in committee. We brought it back in 2020, only to have it tabled due to COVID-19. In 2021, it passed both chambers but was vetoed by Governor Newsom after the Department of General Services raised concerns about implementation being too onerous.

Similar bills to support tropical forests, modeled after ours, have been introduced in the New York legislature. If one passes, we may end up adopting language from it. In the meantime, we sponsored Assemblymember Kalra's request to audit state purchases to understand exactly how many tax dollars are being spent on products that contribute to tropical deforestation, a major driver of climate change and biodiversity loss.

There is no reason for California to take part in destroying the lungs of the earth.

Some years, the biggest challenge is that we're moving multiple bills forward while working to stop bad legislation at the same time. Take 2019. Three monumental bills sponsored by SCIL got signed into law that year. While we were working to change hearts and minds on the topics of fur trapping, circuses, and exotic skins, we also had to fight off the alligator industry as it sought to make California complicit in its cruel and inhumane business.

So when voters on the campaign trail asked if my track record at SCIL was impressive, I felt like saying, you have no idea! We had twenty-two sponsored bills signed into law, many of them copied in other states, which multiplied their impact exponentially. We prevailed despite fierce and relentless opposition from special interests with bottomless pockets and no compunction about spreading misinformation and pressuring lawmakers to stop us in the most unscrupulous ways. We've saved millions of animal lives and an incalculable amount of taxpayer dollars despite their continued attacks and the complexity of getting even the simplest things done in Sacramento.

It was impossible to fit that into an elevator pitch. But some people got the picture and recognized that SCIL was moving mountains.

■ ■ ■

After the epic spay and neuter battle, I was disheartened, exhausted, and, frankly, disgusted by what I had learned about how things get done in Sacramento. We had poured blood, sweat, and tears into a bill that would have saved so many animal lives, only to have our dream ripped away by special interest spending and petty political rivalries.

A lot of people would have walked away at that point. I know that for a fact—I've seen it happen. More than one friend encouraged me to turn my attention to something else. They said it would ruin my life if I stuck with it. That it would eat me alive.

It does take a special level of commitment to get into these kinds of trenches and stay there. Few people or groups will do it. There's a reason SCIL was a pioneer in this space and is pretty much the only nonprofit doing what we do. Dealing with unending frustration and setbacks and incompetence and gameplaying just to get good bills signed into law—it isn't for everyone.

Yet I knew I couldn't let go of the dream. Or it wouldn't let go of me. All of us who had fought to get that bill through had a shared vision. What would happen to it if we walked away? How many more animals would die needlessly in California shelters because we had all moved on to something else? What about my new nonprofit, the network of powerful and like-minded allies we had created? Was all that alliance-building for naught?

I took a few weeks off to process the defeat. Then I got back to work.

■ ■ ■

Los Angeles Mayor Antonio Villaraigosa and the staff at LA Animal Services (LAAS) had gotten to know and really trust me during the AB 1634 fight. We had been able to pass a spay and neuter ordinance in the City of Los Angeles during that time. I was proud to have spearheaded the effort, knowing what a huge difference it would make to the city and that it could serve as a model for others. Now my friends at LAAS had what they said would be an easy task for SCIL.

Based on my experience so far in Sacramento, I knew nothing was easy. But at least this project was straightforward: according to California law, if you wanted to get a license for your dog, you or the vet had to fax the rabies certificate to the city. Paper was the only option (if you can believe that). This truly antiquated way of doing business not only slowed down the licensing process but also discouraged people from going to the trouble in the first place. Who wants to fill in the paperwork online then go fax the certificate separately?

No question about it: if the process were easier, more people would follow it. And more licenses meant more money for shelters and much higher chances of reuniting lost dogs and cats with their families.

Remember, this was before microchipping was common. It would be another eleven years before SCIL got that bill through the legislature. Back then, in 2009, if pets got out and wound up in a shelter, there was a good possibility it would take the families days to track them down, and they might never find them at all.

We needed license tags on as many dogs and cats as possible. To do that, the rabies vaccine verification process had to be simple.

Assembly Bill 2689, the Online Rabies Provision, sponsored by SCIL and authored by Assemblymember Cameron Smyth, was a means of modernizing the state code to specify that public agencies could accept proof of rabies vaccination electronically. People would finally be able to attach a PDF of their pet's rabies certificate to an email instead of needing to fax it.

In essence, we were moving rabies vaccination reporting into the twenty-first century.

A few people started expressing concerns that the bill would require rabies vaccinations every year instead of once every three years. Luckily, it didn't take too much time to dispel the rumors. Once we set the record straight, the bill flew through the Assembly and Senate committees and floor votes with no opposition. Because we had been able to add an urgency clause and secure a two-thirds vote, it went into effect as soon as Governor Schwarzenegger signed it on July 6, 2010.

Getting tags on more dogs made it easier to reunite them with their families. But that was only one facet of the shelter overpopulation problem.

The bigger issue remained: all the backyard breeders operating under the radar and all the people who weren't taking responsibility for their own companion animals. In 2009, State Senator Dean Florez introduced a different version of our spay and neuter bill titled the Pet Responsibility Act, SB 250. Laser-focused on the personal responsibility of pet owners, and designed to save lives and taxpayer dollars, it died in committee. In a rerun of the AB 1634 battle, everybody who made money off animals jumped in to label it a mandatory spay and neuter bill, which it wasn't. They whined about their rights being restricted, when in fact they would simply have been held accountable for the consequences of their actions.

Senator Florez worked tirelessly to educate other lawmakers about all the benefits of the bill. But he couldn't drown out the usual scare tactics. Meanwhile, the pet overpopulation problem kept getting worse. There had to be something we could do.

I'm from Missouri, the Show Me State. Even as a kid, I wanted things to be explained to me with clear facts and hard data. Don't talk to me about miracles, myths, or magic. I don't want to hear about what could happen, in theory, if this one thing goes right and this other thing happens next, and it all falls into place. Let me see exactly what's happening on the ground, then we can talk about what to do about it.

The analytical skills acquired in my career in information technology have proven invaluable in running SCIL. With any problem I'm tackling, I start by looking at the big picture. Then I break it down into smaller pieces to decide the best angle of attack. Most of what we do at SCIL is chip away at problems. Seemingly small advances turn into huge gains over time.

With our second spay and neuter bill DOA and the opposition making clear that it would reserve the same fate for any further efforts, it was time to take a fresh look at the facts we had gathered over the course of this fight.

Fact one: no matter what our opponents said, pet overpopulation was real, and it was causing immense suffering for animals and for the shelter workers and veterinarians in California who were being forced to kill half a million innocent beings a year. Taxpayers were losing out too, to the tune of hundreds of millions of dollars annually. That was the cost of collecting, housing, and euthanizing the animals for which homes couldn't be found.

Fact two: the people and businesses making money off animals, namely, the breeders and pet shop owners, would spend and do whatever it took to keep their profit machine going. Pet overpopulation was not their problem.

Fact three: sometimes the best way to figure out your next move is to listen to your opponents' arguments.

The line of attack we heard most during the spay and neuter battle was that funding for implementation would be hugely unaffordable and complicated. This money angle got hammered over and over again. It went something like this: mandatory sterilization would place an unfair burden on lower-income pet owners who might not know where to get the services, and the whole process would be confusing, unfairly inconvenient, and expensive for them. Many families wouldn't be able to afford the procedure, and they'd be penalized.

None of this was true. Our bill included provisions to address each of these points. But it didn't matter. The opposition had created such a steady drumbeat that sometimes it was all anybody heard. Money, money, money . . . there'd never be enough money to do what we were trying to do. Nonstop fearmongering about how the law would ultimately lead people to not license their dogs, which would in turn create a revenue shortfall for public agencies, which would then put further pressure on animal control departments that were already underfunded and overburdened.

After AB 1634 was killed, several of the staffers and lobbyists I had worked with told me I'd never get anywhere if I didn't address this money question head-on. A sustainable funding mechanism was the best approach. We needed to show that there wouldn't be any cost to taxpayers. It's much harder for lawmakers and the governor to shoot down programs that pay for themselves.

The person who'd helped me the most during the spay and neuter bill was an experienced Sacramento lobbyist with a real soft spot for animals. It was already there when we started working together and I watched it grow as she learned more of the ugly truth of what was happening in shelters. When I mentioned to her that I kept getting this same advice about funding, she suggested that I look into California's specialty license plate program.

This, it turned out, was a brilliant idea. Some of the specialty plates in issue were bringing in as much as $4 million a year, with most of those funds going directly to the causes they were originated for. Monies from our plate would go to spay and neuter services.

It was a different path to the same goal of reducing euthanasia rates in shelters. Problem, meet solution!

Full of enthusiasm and ready to work as hard as necessary to get funds flowing into free and low-cost spay and neuter programs, I waded into a project with no idea that it would consume the next eight years of my life.

By this time, I had seen first-hand how complicated everything is when you're trying to get laws changed. I was about to find out that legislative advocacy is sometimes a cakewalk compared to dealing with the bureaucracy of a state agency that doesn't understand its own programs and procedures.

CHAPTER 4

NAVIGATING A BUREAUCRATIC HOUSE OF MIRRORS

The principle behind specialty license plates is simple: people pay to switch out a standard Department of Motor Vehicles (DMV) plate for one showing their support for a specific cause. A portion of the fees generated goes to that cause.

The first plate launched through the program in California hit the road in 1993. Titled "Coastline," it features a sunset and palm tree design by iconic pop artist Wayne Thiebaud. Proceeds go to the California Arts Council. You still see this gorgeous plate throughout the state today. It has raised tens of millions for the arts, and currently brings in about $2.5 million a year. The program got a big boost from the Million Plates campaign launched by the California Arts Council with help from Governor Arnold Schwarzenegger and First Lady Maria Shriver, with the aim of raising $40 million for arts funding. Through this campaign, they emphasized that specialty plates continue to fund programs regardless of what happens to the state's budget.

Exactly the kind of stability we needed for spay and neuter programs.

Other plates followed after "Coastline," and the program built real momentum until an anti-abortion group tried to get a plate with a graphic image on it approved in the late 1990s. Lawsuits followed. There's always someone to ruin a good thing for everyone else. The political plate project got stopped, and multiple safeguards were put into place to nip controversial designs in the bud. First, proponents needed to find a sponsor, meaning a state agency that agreed to administer and oversee it. The thinking was that some fringe group might get thousands of like-minded supporters to say they'd buy a certain plate, but it wouldn't be able to find a state agency to go along with the plan. Second, once they got the design approved, proponents had to get 7,500 preorders.

I understand that these kinds of protections are necessary. There's enough road rage in this country as it is—we don't need license plates setting people off too. But for a new nonprofit raising money for a truly good cause, the requirements seemed like an impossible mountain to climb.

When I started looking into the project in earnest in 2008, there were eleven specialty plates in circulation. It had been more than ten years since a new one was approved.

I made up my mind that our spay and neuter plate would be the first to be greenlighted in the twenty-first century.

I had known US Senator Alex Padilla since his time on the Los Angeles City Council when we'd team up to organize spay days in his district. A real animal lover, Senator Padilla had supported many of my initiatives in meaningful ways. He understood at a deep level how bad the situation was in shelters and how important it was to reduce the suffering that was happening there. In addition, he had a front-row seat to the AB 1634 saga, since he was floor manager on the day the State Senate killed the bill. I knew he'd be eager to help if we had a really good idea for tackling this problem from a different angle.

Senator Padilla spoke plainly: he loved the idea, but he couldn't do anything for us until we had a sponsoring agency. That needed to be our first order of business.

The California Veterinary Medical Board (VMB) seemed the logical place to start. Veterinarians are on the frontlines of the euthanasia tragedy, and they're as anxious as anyone to find a solution. VMB members Linda Starr and Dr. Stephanie Ferguson both expressed interest right away. Executive Officer Susan Geranen was especially excited. She became a driving force throughout the process. The late Dr. Tom Kendall, a prominent Sacramento veterinarian, had given heart-touching testimony for our spay and neuter bill, so it was easy to bring him along too. This was the first time I'd ever interacted with the VMB as an agency. Its early support for the spay and neuter plate program spoke volumes about its commitment to saving animal lives. A few years later, I had the honor of being appointed to the VMB by Speaker John Perez as a public member in 2010, and to serve two full terms until 2018.

Once we had an agency behind us, then-State Senator Padilla helped set up a meeting with administrators from the DMV to establish exactly what we needed to do to get a new plate on the road.

Remember, this was the first time the DMV had processed a request like ours in more than a decade.

To our dismay, we quickly understood that the administrators were figuring things out as they went. We'd hear one thing on

Monday and something else on Tuesday. Hard as we tried to ask the right questions, we couldn't get straight answers. The goalposts were moving constantly. Naïvely, we assumed a state agency would have set rules for participating in state programs and that we'd walk out of that first meeting with a to-do list. Instead, we felt like we'd stepped into a house of mirrors.

After multiple meetings and weeks of waiting, we were finally able to get a handle on what was required of us just to get started. Step one: set up yet another nonprofit specifically for the plate. Step two: get the proposed design approved by the California Highway Patrol (to ensure the plate was readable). Step three: secure 7,500 preorders within one year.

Okay, it was a lot, but at least we knew what we had to do. By the time we got these marching orders, it was 2010!

■ ■ ■

Very early on, I talked about the plate idea with my friend Keely Shaye Brosnan. I met Keely shortly after moving to California in the late 1980s. We lived next door to one another in Hollywood and became fast friends. She hadn't met her future husband, Pierce Brosnan, yet. Keely was working as an environmental correspondent on ABC's *The Home Show*. It was supposed to be about all things domestic with some environmental news thrown in, but Keely was always pitching animal rights stories since that was one of her passions. Her work was so good that her producers let her do it. She'd put together compelling pieces about the mistreatment of greyhounds or farm animals and drop the VHS cassettes off at my apartment with a note that said, "Watch this!"

Well, I did watch, and it changed the course of my life.

Growing up in an Italian household in Missouri, my family ate meat dishes all the time. It was all so normal. But something about it never felt right to me. One time, at the age of around ten, riding in the back of my parents' Dodge Polara, we pulled up next to a cattle truck full of cows. I asked where the cows were going. My dad said they were being sent to slaughter "so you can have your hamburgers." I was so confused and horrified. That memory still pains me. I *knew* in my heart there was no difference between those animals and us humans, that they shouldn't be treated like they didn't have feelings or didn't count. But, like many people today, I didn't know I had choices. I was trapped in the lies we were taught as kids about the four food groups and the need to get protein from animals.

I'd stopped eating red meat about a decade before watching Keely's videos, for nutritional reasons. Now I knew I could no longer justify eating any meat or dairy. It was also around that time that I read John Robbins's book *Diet for a New America*, which clearly shows the nexus between animal suffering on factory farms, the health problems humans experience when they consume animal products, and all the environmental damage that is occurring because of people's refusal to change their diet.

I became a vegetarian immediately and was full vegan within a few years. That was over three decades ago, and I've never looked back.

It was Keely who introduced me to the legislative side of activism. In 2005, she and Pierce were heavily involved in the Heritage Tree Preservation Act, or Senate Bill 1799. Majestic old-growth trees that had been in the ground since 1852 or earlier, and were thus at least as old as California, were getting chopped down left and right. The bill was part of a multiyear effort to stop this destruction of the state's heritage. It had failed in the Assembly by just two votes in 2004 and was being reintroduced by Senate President Pro Tempore Don Perata.

This was my first experience seeing up close how much power special interests have and how determined they are to protect those interests at all costs. Under unrelenting pressure from all sides, the bill had been watered down to the point that protections would only apply to trees on nonfederal forestlands in California, including land owned by timber companies. Well, those companies weren't going to quietly accept even minimal restrictions on their activities, heritage or not.

It was an epic fight.

I attended a big fundraiser on the garden patio at AXE Restaurant in Venice. About two hundred people came, including many celebrities. At the end of the event, Keely told me they needed to do a press conference at the Capitol to save those trees and asked if I could facilitate. Of course! I had never done anything like that before, but reckoned I could figure it out. Jump in and learn how to swim has been one of the major themes of my life, and I wouldn't have it any other way.

Senator Perata's staff helped me put together the list of lawmakers to contact. Anyone who's ever done cold calling will tell you it's not easy and it's no fun. But I have to admit, fewer people hang up on you when you can drop the name of a James Bond actor in your intro.

I arrived at the Capitol in a limousine with Keely and Pierce. So many people were waiting; it was hard to know who was there for the trees and who just wanted to meet Pierce. We made our way through the crowd and into Senator Perata's office. Soon the Legislative Women's Caucus showed up, ostensibly to hear about the bill, but they also seemed giddy about seeing Pierce. Senator Liz Figueroa, the caucus chair, was the first one in the door, all business while introducing herself.

I still can't believe that bill was defeated. Irreplaceable trees sacrificed for special interests that had access to other forest resources? How can that be? I learned, maybe for the first time, but certainly not the last, that really important bills die if enough money and special interests line up against them.

That campaign to protect the old-growth trees was a once-in-a-lifetime opportunity for me to build relationships with the movers and shakers who get things done, both in Hollywood and Sacramento. Having celebrities in your corner changes everything. It's been one of SCIL's greatest resources from the beginning. A lot of big stars are glad to use their big platforms to help animals.

■ ■ ■

Keely loved the spay and neuter license plate idea. To my surprise, she immediately suggested that I ask Pierce about creating the artwork. Pierce is an artist, but few people knew that at the time. He shared his work only with friends and family. I loved his art and had had giclée prints made of a few of his pieces.

One night over dinner, I mentioned to Pierce that we needed a design for our new license plate, and that Keely thought he might be interested. He was curious and asked a lot of questions. I explained how the whole process would work, that the design would need to be approved and then we'd have to meet a high bar for preorders. Understandably, he said he'd need some time to think about it. What a gift when he called a few days later to say he was excited about the project and that his creative process was already underway.

After we worked out the details, things on his side went quiet for a while, which had me biting my nails. I was over the moon to have someone as talented and famous as Pierce do the artwork, but I also knew how busy he was. When would he find time to send over proofs?

As it turned out, Pierce was quiet because he was doing iteration after iteration, trying to get the graphics just right. Boy, was it worth the wait. The final design was better than I could have imagined. Pierce called it Wise Dog and Cool Cat. It features the sweet Abyssinian he and Keely had at the time, Angel Baby, as well as their rescue dog Shilo, a real sweetheart we all adored. The blue bone pictured is the one Shilo used to carry around everywhere. The depiction of those two fur babies is a love letter to all animals, and the rays of sunshine rising up behind them are a celebration of California.

Pierce donated the design in perpetuity, meaning the plate could stay on the road and keep generating funds for spay and neuter programs forever.

Promoting the plate with *Grey's Anatomy* actor Justin Chambers, LA Mayor Antonio Villaraigosa, Pierce Brosnan, and Assemblymember Richard Alarcon.

We had a sponsoring agency behind us and a fantastic plate design approved. We had set up the proper legal structure and bank account to receive funds. Then came the moment of truth: we had twelve months to get 7,500 people to preorder the plate.

In June of 2010, we held a kickoff press conference at the West LA Animal Shelter. Pierce and Keely were there, along with then-mayor Antonio Villaraigosa and city councilmembers, former model and *Grey's Anatomy* actor Justin Chambers, journalist Lu Parker, and a host of people from the VMB. All the local channels covered the conference.

What a delight to see so many people in attendance and so much excitement. It was go time.

■ ■ ■

Once word started getting out about the new plate and where the proceeds would go, orders flowed in. Our hopes were high, but the logistics were their own kind of nightmare since I was solely responsible for keeping track of the orders. People would fill out the forms and mail us everything, including their credit card information or a check. My home turned into a processing center. Mountains of papers and folders piled up everywhere. All the information that came in through the different channels during the day had to be entered into a massive spreadsheet at night—by me. And it had to be reconciled constantly, as folks were always making changes, moving, cancelling, even dying. The work never ended. My then-husband had a full-time job and helped with the project as he could on nights and weekends. We never took a break because there was no time. Pure insanity when I look back, but who else was going to do it?

SCIL had built up a long list of supporters during the spay and neuter saga, so we had that group of like-minded friends to tap into. These were people who fully understood the extent of the shelter death problem and the importance of what we were doing. Many are still supporting SCIL today. Everyone at LA City Hall was immensely helpful as well.

By any measure, we were off to a good start.

After a few months, we reached a plateau in orders, and began to have doubts about whether we could get the momentum back. Anyone who's ever gathered signatures, even for a very popular cause, knows the feeling. At first, it seems like everyone you talk to responds favorably to your pitch. Then at one point you get the impression that everyone you talk to is either not interested or has already signed. It felt like we were approaching that stage. To convince those who weren't familiar with the project or the issue, we had to explain the whole program and get them to trust us enough to give us their personal information and prepay for a plate that didn't yet exist.

In April 2012, we stalled at about 4,000 preorders and a little more than $275,000 collected. Assemblymember Jose Solorio threw us a lifeline by carrying Assembly Bill 610, which gave us an extra year to get the requisite number of preorders. He did a great job explaining the vital role the plate would play in bringing funds to low- and no-cost spay and neuter programs. His bill passed both houses unanimously, and Governor Jerry Brown signed it in May.

One more year added to the clock.

To kick off this next phase, we organized a big event in a West Los Angeles Petco to promote the plate. It was quite a star-studded affair. Pierce was there, along with Governor Brown and "First Dog" Sutter. Assemblymember Solorio came with LA City

Me with Assemblymember Jose Solorio, Pierce Brosnan, Cesar Millan, and Congressman Tony Cardenas.

Governor Jerry Brown helping us promote the plate with Pierce Brosnan, me, First Dog Sutter, and Cesar Millan.

Councilmember (and future congressman) Tony Cardenas, who had been my primary contact at the LA City Council for all things related to animals. He brought Cesar Millan, whose show *Dog Whisperer* was in its eighth year on the air. Cesar's attendance attracted a whole new audience.

All this star power gave us a fresh shot of enthusiasm, but we still needed money to get the word out. Dr. Michelson came to the rescue once again. California's insanely high shelter death rates weighed heavily on his heart, and he was doing everything in his power to get money flowing to spay and neuter programs through the plate. To keep our effort going, he provided funding for the printing and shipping of promotional brochures, assistance with order-taking and processing, plus the cash we needed, at just the right time. His support allowed us to get brochures into vet offices across the state. Petco also agreed to display them at checkouts everywhere in California, which helped immensely.

In January 2013, we hit 7,500 preorders. The bank account we had set up for the fund had swelled to $487,000.

At our press conference in Los Angeles to secure the last orders needed to get the plate on the road. From left to right are Lisa Avery, Dr. Gary Michelson, Dr. Tom Kendall, Dr. Richard Johnson, Assemblymember Jose Solorio, Pierce Brosnan, me, Cesar Millan, Congressman Tony Cardenas, Linda Starr, and Dr. Stephanie Ferguson.

The day of my fiftieth birthday was the same day that I wired that full amount to the DMV, along with the spreadsheet I'd been maintaining for years with all the preorder details. We had pulled it off. Money was going to start flowing regularly into programs to address California's pet overpopulation problem.

Best birthday gift ever, right?

■ ■ ■

The joy was short-lived. I soon learned that the DMV was still using computer code from the 1980s. That perfect spreadsheet I kept so painstakingly? The DMV didn't have a way to upload it, meaning it all had to be entered manually into its dinosaur system.

Over the next nine months, I met regularly with top administrators from the State of California and the DMV as they tried to figure out how to get our plate on the road. Molehills became mountains. If someone in the spreadsheet had made a mistake filling out their current plate number, the order got blocked. Same thing if their tag had expired. A few people had moved and forgotten to update their address. That created its own set of problems. The smallest discrepancy could trigger a chain reaction.

We had to wait for every one of the DMV-side details to get ironed out before we could send the plate to production. Multiple samples of the plate had to be produced. It took months and months to get the final approval.

This whole saga put an immense strain on my personal life and relationships with the people who supported me. There were times when they had serious doubts about whether this thing was ever going to get done. In my mind, that meant they were doubting me, and it was painful. We were dealing with such an arcane and inefficient system that every step forward was followed by two steps back, and there wasn't anything we could do to speed up the process.

In September 2013, the very first "Pet Lover's Specialty License Plate" was shipped to its new owner—me! Three cars later, I still get a feeling of pride driving around with it. When people comment on the plate, I smile and say it was a labor of love. They just don't know how much labor it took.

Over the following years, the program hit a few more speed bumps that caused us major headaches and substantial delays, but luckily didn't send us back to square one.

I was on the Veterinary Medical Board in 2013, and we were tasked with writing the regulations about where the funds raised would go and how they would be distributed. We submitted our proposal to the Office of Administrative Law (OAL), and in

2014, got a twenty-two-page denial letter, outlining a list of reasons why the distribution system we had proposed was not acceptable.

After crossing every "t" and dotting every "i," we were still discovering new rules no one had ever told us about, and many that were being made up along the way.

We sponsored a bill in 2015 to address the concerns raised by OAL. It passed, but that wasn't the end of our troubles, by a long stretch. The funds were available for distribution, technically, but now we were being told the VMB could not be our sponsoring agency since spay and neuter surgeries were performed by veterinarians, which created an inherent conflict of interest.

Kafka couldn't have scripted it better.

My lobbyist suggested that the most logical agency to manage the plate was the California Department of Food and Agriculture (CDFA), since it was already administering a different plate fund and had grant programs.

CDFA serves the interests of big agriculture, so it wasn't a natural fit for an organization that promotes animal welfare and veganism like SCIL. But by that time, I just wanted things to move forward. Thus began the unnecessarily complicated and drawn-out process of dealing with that new agency. My emails went unanswered. It was impossible to get a face-to-face meeting. And it went on like this for years!

Finally, in 2017, Senate Bill 673 officially transferred oversight of the Pet Lover's License Plate Program from the VMB to CDFA, which, for better or worse, still has that responsibility today.

■ ■ ■

In 2018, like every year, CDFA had a budget for grants. Yet the grant administrator it hired failed to include our spay and neuter nonprofit in its decision-making. In fact, there was almost no communication with us at all. We had to fight for every scrap of information we got, even though SB 673 specifically stipulated that we were to be consulted in all processes.

Another layer of complication: CDFA still wasn't collaborating with our nonprofit on establishing grant criteria. Instead, it had appointed a panel of anonymous reviewers who followed a nontransparent process to award grants. It came to light at one point that some of the fake animal welfare groups SCIL was constantly at odds with had infiltrated these panels and were involved in

At the Joint Legislative Audit Committee hearing, delighted that the concerns we had raised about processes and the distribution of funds were now going to be analyzed and documented. On my right is Dr. Allan Drusys. On my left is the chief consultant of the Senate Business and Professions Committee, Bill Gage. On his left is Assemblymember Bill Quirk.

deciding where funds should go. When announcing its first grant program, CDFA declared that it had $330,000 to give. We had been told the fund had over a million dollars.

Transparency is key not only to keeping a program like this running, but also to maintaining public trust. At this point, even *our* trust was wearing thin.

It was time for fresh eyes on CDFA's administration of the fund.

In August of 2019, at the urging of SCIL, Assemblymember Bill Quirk submitted a request for the California State Auditor to formally review how CDFA was administering and accounting for the funds. His request passed the Joint Legislative Audit Committee (JLAC) with unanimous, bipartisan support from committee members from both houses. Legislators understood the urgency of the request. JLAC is one of the bodies that works as intended in Sacramento. The audit was given priority and was completed within a year.

Once the findings were published, CDFA became very responsive. We discovered that it had over $1.6 million ready for distribution, whereas a few months before, we were told it had $330,000!

The JLAC audit was just what the doctor ordered. It delivered transparency and change.

Today, the program works as it's supposed to. Tracking the money that flows into and out of the fund is easy. As I write, CDFA has granted out over $2 million for spay and neuter surgeries in underserved communities.

All the headaches and the heartbreaks were worth it.

CHAPTER 5

DINING WITH DOGS FROM COAST TO COAST

While the license plate program was coming together, pieces of my world were falling apart. My mother passed away in 2012, at the age of eighty-seven. She was a rock in my life, my best friend. At least once a week, we'd hop on the phone to catch up on each other's lives. I so admired her spirit and her wisdom. While she'd never been an activist for a cause like mine, she knew more about hard work than anyone. I think that's one of the reasons she was so proud and supportive of everything I was doing. She knew how much commitment it took.

Mom had more intuition than anyone I've known. Somehow, she could always sense what was going on with me and get me to open up in ways no one else could. That would help me process whatever was happening and keep moving forward. And she was wise—one of those people who get better with age because they

Me and my mom, Jean Mancuso, visiting her parents' hometown of Casteltermini, Sicily, in the early 90s.

keep learning and growing. I'd like to think I inherited that quality.

Toward the end of 2013, my marriage of twenty years ended unexpectedly. When something like that happens, so many people say, "You must have known." They assume there were all kinds of signs everywhere that you didn't see. But that's not always true. In my case, one day we were working together on all these animal projects and talking about life goals that we seemed to be totally aligned on. The next, I was pulling up in front of my house in the middle of a workday to see him standing in the driveway, looking distraught, warning me not to go inside. I assumed the worst, that something had happened to one of our animals. That wasn't why he didn't want me to go into the house. It was because he had moved his stuff out.

"You're leaving me?" I asked.

He handed me the file he was holding and said, "I want a divorce."

I cried off and on for the next nine months. It was hard to get out of bed. Friends in LA were encouraging me to move back there from Laguna Beach, about an hour away, to get a fresh start. My sister in Napa kept telling me how beautiful Northern California was and how great it would be to live close to one another again.

All I wanted to do was hunker down with my animals and let the world go by.

Grief is a tricky thing. A lot of people get stuck in it. I've seen it with my own eyes. Friends who've turned to alcohol or drugs. Or they start spending all their time fixated on how unfair it is that this one thing happened, and it becomes all they want to talk about. It's possible to remain in that space for a long time. Even forever. Some people just accept that a particular event is the beginning of their demise, and that's the path they stay on.

Fortunately, for me, the day came when some light started filtering into that dark place where I was stuck. Don't get me wrong, I still considered his actions to be a complete betrayal of trust, and they left a deep scar on me. But over time, I began to understand that a lot of people have been blindsided by their partner up and walking out on them. I was lucky in so many ways. It could have been much, much worse. With some hard work, I'd be able to keep my home. I was healthy. I had wonderful family and friends who supported me through thick and thin. I had animals that I loved, and who needed me. Crucially, I had a purpose: all the animals I had helped and all the ones I was going to help. Who would do that work if I shrank into my sadness and stayed there? Would they stop having a voice because I couldn't figure out how to transform my grief?

The lobbyist I'd been working with for five years in Sacramento knew what I was going through. She gave me some time to process the losses, then set to work getting me motivated again. Looking back, I'm grateful for her message: momentum is hard to gain and easy to lose. When you've got it, you need to do whatever it takes to maintain it. That reputation I had worked so hard to acquire as someone who knew how to get things done and never gave up would evaporate if I stayed off the grid too long.

We came up with a plan to keep me in the game with a bill that would be important but not too heavy of a political lift.

Here's how it started.

During the license plate saga, my husband and I had adopted two wonderful little chihuahuas named Candy and Dinky. These sweet dogs had been literally thrown out on the street and left to die by a breeder in Hollywood. A neighbor saw the whole thing go down and ran over to confront him.

"What are you doing?" she yelled.

"I'm done with them," the breeder snapped.

"But they could get hit by a car!"

"Not my problem," he said, and went back inside.

I'd watched that same scenario play out over and over again with backyard breeders like this monster who had no regard for the animals. How many times had I stood outside a shelter and seen a hobby breeder pull in the parking lot, pop the hatch, and unload a litter of puppies or kittens that didn't come out quite right. Maybe their legs were too short. Or their fur was too long. Anything the breeder saw as an imperfection could be a death sentence. If the whole litter got sick with a treatable illness, these breeders would pack them up and dump them at the shelter to avoid veterinary bills.

The neighbor took the chihuahuas back to her house and started calling rescue groups. My good friend and founding SCIL board member Haze Lynn wound up taking them in through her rescue organization and finding them a forever home. With us, in Laguna. I still tear up when I think about those two amazing little soulmates who meant the world to me.

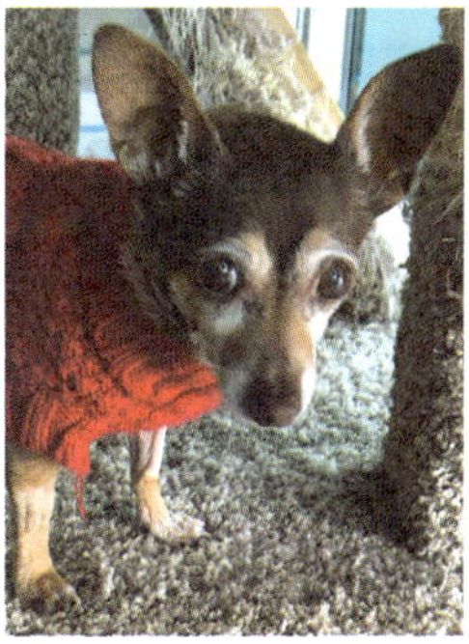

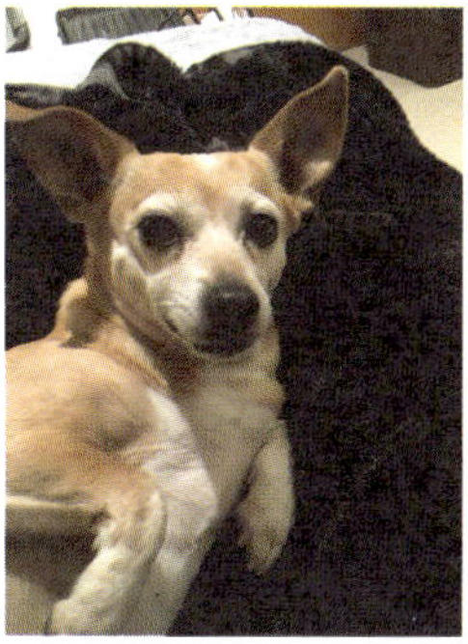

My canine soulmates, Dinky Pooh and Candy.

One day, not long after we adopted Candy and Dinky, we took them to a Veggie Grill restaurant. I was waiting outside while my husband went inside to order when a manager rushed over to inform me that dogs weren't allowed on the patio. I thought I must have misheard. We'd taken them to a different location of that same chain just a few weeks earlier. Now we were being asked to leave.

The manager who came to break the news to me obviously didn't think much of the rule.

"Sorry, state law," he shrugged. "Can't have dogs where food is being consumed."

"Well, that's a law that needs to be changed," I responded.

We got our order to-go and I ate mine at the computer, looking for the law in question. There it was: a clause in the California Retail Food Code prohibited bringing live animals to dining establishments. Even if restaurants wanted to, they weren't allowed to open their outdoor areas to dogs. A lot of dog owners and restaurants took their chances, hoping they wouldn't get caught. But they were still breaking the law.

Flash forward a year: my lobbyist reminded me of this story, and suggested that this be our next bill.

Assemblymember Mariko Yamada and I had developed a working relationship during the fight over the spay and neuter bill. She had voted against it because she represented agriculture interests in Napa Valley. But she offered to help with future animal-related bills as long as they weren't controversial and didn't upset the farming community. This one was a pretty easy sell. Plus, her district is also a hospitality hub.

She introduced AB 1965 in February of 2014. It gave restaurants the option to welcome dogs as long as certain conditions were met. Eating areas needed to be kept clean, sidewalks had to comply with local ordinances, and dogs had to be kept on a leash or in a carrier. Basic rules that nobody would argue with. Local governments could add additional standards if they wanted to.

It was a win for everyone. Public health officials had more time to focus on more important work. Animal-loving restaurant owners had the option to welcome four-legged patrons. And of course, the millions of people who like to include their dogs on a family night out could finally do so without worrying about getting kicked out.

No matter what you try to do in Sacramento, you're going to have some naysayers. In this case, we mostly had to spend time reassuring the California Restaurant Association and the Department of Public Health that our bill wouldn't entail any costs or add to anyone's workload. Nor would restaurants be forced to accommodate dogs if they didn't want to—they'd simply have guidelines in case they did.

Popular legislation is hard to fight, and we didn't encounter too much resistance. I think the Restaurant Association was ready for the bill. They knew it would be good for business and they got their members on board quickly. I imagine there were lots of dog lovers among them.

We figured the media would lap up the story, and we weren't disappointed. Once the bill had passed both chambers and was awaiting the governor's signature, Assemblymember Yamada put out a statement thanking her colleagues for "allowing Californians to enjoy noodles with their poodles." She wished everyone "bone appétit," and several major news outlets ran with that headline. Even *The Economist* got in on the action, printing a delightful cartoon with that caption, showing dogs being treated like royalty at a very upscale restaurant.

It was the kind of light-hearted story people love, and just what I needed after a very trying year.

■ ■ ■

One of the people who helped me document the reality in animal shelters during the spay and neuter bill was Sandra Mohr. A well-known animal rights documentarian, Sandra was my friend Jane Velez-Mitchell's partner at the time. In the shelters we visited, she would film the interviews I conducted with staff and veterinarians and try to capture the conditions the animals were living in. Anytime I got overwhelmed with emotion, Sandra would step in and keep the show going.

One day, while we were on our way to a shoot at the Madera facility, a stray min-pin darted by our car in a complete panic. We pulled over and started running after it, making our mission to get it to safety, which was no easy feat, as she was putting every ounce of energy in that little body into not getting caught. At one point, I found myself in the middle of the road, directing traffic, even stopping an eighteen-wheeler that was headed right for the dog.

People told me later it was a scene meant for late-night news. *Woman doing report on shelter shuts down freeway offramp and stops big rig to save stray dog!*

A young passerby I'd recruited to the effort ended up successfully cornering the pooch.

We brought the min-pin over to our car, capturing the whole thing on video. The second she was inside, you could see the fear and panic leave her body. She let out a deep breath and settled into my lap. Who knows how long she'd been out on the street, fending for herself.

Well, her fate certainly changed that day, when Sandra sent the video to Jane. Before you knew it, "Foxy" was in her new digs in Los Angeles with Jane and Sandra and a number of other rescues, living the best of all lives.

Jane and I had known one another since the 1990s, when we met at a vegan Thanksgiving meal. But we became the closest of friends from the day she took in Foxy.

The following year, Jane moved to New York and got her own show on HLN, a subsidiary of CNN, but we stayed in close touch. When she heard the Dining with Dogs bill was making its way through the legislature, she insisted on having me on to talk about it. Turns out the issue had been on her mind too, ever since a vegan restaurant she'd invested in, run by a management team that was hypervigilant about food safety, got a B grade. Jane was shocked, especially when she learned that it was because a very small dog had squeezed through the wrought iron fence onto the patio while the health inspectors were on-site. Vegan restaurants were getting harassed from all sides due to the threat they posed to long-established eateries serving meat and dairy. Jane figured politics had something to do with the grade. Whatever the reason, she shared my conviction that the law needed to change in New York too.

I went on for a live interview in August. The CNN studio in Hollywood places guests in a dark room with the camera very close to their face and a monitor showing what's happening on the air. As I sat watching Jane start the show on the other side of the country, waiting for my turn to go on, my phone pinged. I leaned out of the frame to read the text message.

JERRY BROWN JUST SIGNED THE BILL.

Talk about timing!

News anchors love to say "Breaking News." That night, Jane wasn't exaggerating. Her viewers were the first to hear about this sea change in California. The whole culture around dining out and welcoming animals as family members shifted massively.

Right there, in front of her audience, Jane said I needed to come do the same bill in New York.

Nothing like the pressure of being asked to do something on live TV. Of course I said yes, not expecting Jane to follow up right away. But she did, a few weeks later, then again a few weeks after that. I explained that I'd never done any kind of legislative work in New York and had no idea where to begin. She promised to help.

Next thing I knew, I was on a plane to New York to meet with Linda Rosenthal, the assemblymember representing Manhattan and a well-known animal rights champion, to see if she would carry the bill. I also interviewed lobbyists to see if they were a good fit for this statewide campaign. Assemblymember Rosenthal introduced the bill in March of 2015. Legislators offered their support quickly, as they had in California, but the New York City health department started lobbying heavily against the bill right away. Our lobbyists and Assemblymember Rosenthal's stellar staff took meeting after meeting with public health officials to address each point they raised. For a while, we were worried that their concerns about safety would sink the bill. But we persevered, and we prevailed. In October, Governor Andrew Cuomo signed A05956 into law, giving New Yorkers the right to dine with their canine companions in outdoor areas.

Sometimes bills are just common sense. Of course, people should be able to dine with their dogs outdoors.

After AB 1965 was introduced in California, I contacted Veggie Grill to let them know the experience I had at one of their restaurants was the inspiration for the bill. They were so excited they made me a brand ambassador. I received a giant stack of gift cards in the mail. What fun I had handing those out to people in Sacramento while pitching the bill. Vegan food and dogs—what a great combo!

So many people take it for granted that they can eat outdoors with their dogs. Like most things, it's an option today because at some point, someone—in this case, SCIL—put in the work to make it possible.

■ ■ ■

Another major success was in store for us in 2015 with the passage of Assembly Concurrent Resolution 56. Authored by Assemblymember Erick Linder, ACR 56 made the shelter animal the official pet of the state of California. While this might seem like just a symbolic thing, it was actually a big deal. It gave lawmakers and local governments permission to highlight through their offices the work being done by animal services and humane societies.

While considerable strides had been made thanks to SCIL and the other wonderful groups working to reduce pet overpopulation, public and private shelters were still taking in over 800,000 animals a year and euthanizing more than half of them. Most of the animals being killed were healthy and adoptable. Meanwhile, people continued to order designer dogs over the internet like they were ordering pairs of shoes.

We needed to shed more light on the problem and get more allies on our side. Awareness is key, along with education, which we promote too, with considerable support from legislators.

ACR 56 is one of our low-profile, high-impact successes. Because a big part of the work we do focuses on changing the culture, helping people see companion animals not as disposable possessions or status symbols but rather as wonderful, sentient beings that, if given a chance, will enhance human lives in ways that cannot be imagined, no matter what they look like or where they come from. By making the shelter animal its official symbol, the state of California was making a statement. Saying yes, we're proud to be affiliated with these animals. They are *our* animals. And we're going to do everything we can to spread the word about how awesome they are and how much help they need.

It was the ultimate invitation to adopt.

Two years later, in 2017, we would face our biggest battle yet in getting California pet stores on board to help tackle the animal shelter crisis.

Spoiler alert: they didn't come willingly.

CHAPTER 6

BRINGING ANIMALS INTO PRESIDENTIAL POLITICS

"Want to meet Hillary Clinton?"

"Are you kidding me? Where? When? Of course!"

"Come up to Hollywood right now. The event starts in three hours."

The call came out of the blue early in May 2016 from Simone Reyes, then in her second year as a SCIL board member. Simone had moved to California from New York in 2012 and was quickly adopted by the animal rights community. Everyone could see she was the real deal. I met her at a PETA event in 2015 and thought, *Who is this person everyone seems to know?* Turns out Simone has real creds. She'd opened the Animal Rights National Conference multiple times and has a TEDx talk on animal rights that's been viewed more than 200,000 times.

No wonder all the animal rights groups were courting her. Luckily for me, Simone felt SCIL was the best fit for her. We're both staunch vegans (not even the smallest exceptions, ever), huge fans of the band The Stray Cats (what can I say?), and firm believers that in certain areas, including animal rights, the only way to get people to consistently do the right thing is to pass laws that make it illegal to do the wrong thing.

From 2015 on, any time I talk about what "we" did, it includes Simone. She's someone who suits up and shows up for the animals—and for SCIL—every time she's needed.

Simone had been working for over thirty years with Russell Simmons, one of the event hosts and emcee for the Hillary Clinton event. It was going to be a star-studded affair with Mary J. Blige performing and countless celebrities attending. A committed vegan and animal rights champion, Russell had rescinded his endorsement of Senator Bernie Sanders's campaign for the Democratic presidential nomination a few months prior, partly because of Bernie's refusal to take a tough stance against big ag. He then endorsed Secretary Clinton and planned the fundraiser Simone was calling about.

I wasn't exactly invited, so the truth would need to be stretched a bit to get me in.

When you have eight animals in your care like I did, you don't often decide on a whim to make a two-hour trip to an event you may or may not be allowed to attend. But this was the opportunity of a lifetime. I made arrangements with a neighbor to feed the dogs and cats, agonized over what to wear, then launched into the Southern California afternoon traffic.

Thankfully, Russell was able to pull some strings. Before I knew it, I was in a small backstage area, secured by the secret service, with Simone, Russell, his girlfriend, one of his assistants, the mayor of Los Angeles, a handful of celebrities, Clinton's longtime aide Huma Abedin, and Secretary Clinton herself. We whispered to Huma that there was a voting block the campaign was neglecting to target: all the single-issue voters like us who had no idea how good Clinton's record was on animals. Could we possibly get just a moment of the secretary's time?

We almost fainted when she said yes.

Next thing we knew, Hillary Clinton was standing there, chatting with us, telling us about how much she loved elephants, and how much she liked the idea of including animal rights in her platform. Did I have a card I could leave with her?

My hands were shaking so badly I could barely get my purse open.

Figuring this would just be another great story to tell, I gave her my card, thanked her again, and left.

A week later, Sara Jacobs, then a policy advisor on Clinton's campaign and today a US representative, called to ask if I would help prepare an animal rights page for the issues website.

"It would be the honor of my life," I said. And it was true.

Within a few short months, a new "Protecting Animals and Wildlife" position paper was posted to the Clinton campaign website, outlining proposed protections for public lands, wildlife, pets and domesticated animals, farm animals, and horses. To our delight, the secretary went even further, talking about her strong history of standing up for animal rights.

■ ■ ■

From the day I started getting involved in this work in California, joining Sue and Kevin Walshe's Animal Rescue Foundation of Dana Point back in 1995, long before legislative advocacy was even on my radar, I would watch politicians talk about all the problems that needed to be addressed in the world without ever mentioning animals, even in passing. I found it unacceptable. Bringing animals into the public conversation became one of my personal goals.

My heart skipped a beat the day I stood in the press room with Los Angeles Mayor Antonio Villaraigosa and heard him talk about dogs, cats, and shelter euthanasia rates in his speech. It was 2008, and LA had just adopted the spay and neuter ordinance I helped spearhead. A watershed moment for those of us who had been working in the shadows for the animals and only making slow progress because our issue wasn't on the public's mind.

Another huge milestone came in 2010, when I helped lead the effort to stop the US from getting behind the plan the International Whaling Commission (IWC) had come up with to allow some countries to resume killing whales for profit. It was just two years into President Obama's first term, and his administration had pledged to support the proposal. The IWC's argument was that the best way to save these magnificent creatures wasn't to end commercial whaling altogether, but rather to regulate how they were killed. It represented a major step backward, one that we all expected President Obama to reject, based on what he had said on the campaign trail.

Keely Brosnan arranged a meeting at the Santa Monica office of the Natural Resources Defense Council (NRDC) with Joel Reynolds, now the NRDC's Western director. I invited SCIL supporter Dr. Michelson to join us, and of course he found time. We were all feeling so betrayed and were absolutely determined to stop this reversal from happening.

After several hours of brainstorming, we came up with a plan for a media push that would get the issue in front of the president. Pierce would do a short video, looking straight into the camera and asking President Obama to honor his campaign promise to protect marine life, including by ending whaling.

From there, the pieces fell into place quickly. The International Fund for Animal Welfare offered to make the video. Keely and I secured funding from a handful of national animal rights groups to cover the production costs. We were confident about our chances for success. A strong message delivered by Pierce was bound to make for a great ad campaign.

What happened next boosted our impact exponentially: Longtime animal rights champion John Paul DeJoria offered to give our campaign TV advertising slots he had secured for his Patrón tequila brand, free of charge. Our video ended up getting more airtime than we could have ever imagined, much less paid for ourselves. At the same time, Dr. Michelson and I led a campaign to get ads in all the major news outlets in Washington, DC. Every time the president turned on the TV or opened a newspaper, he'd see our message about not selling out the whales.

Pierce sent a letter directly to the administration, using 007 language to implore President Obama not to give whalers from Japan, Norway, and Iceland a "license to kill" the whales.

"'Change we can believe in' can and should extend beyond America's shores to benefit the whales," it read. "At a time when wildlife is being decimated along America's southeast coast, it's probably a good time to reflect on the disasters that humans can visit on the welfare of the planet."

Being called out by James Bond prompted President Obama to act. He ended up taking diplomatic measures against the countries that weren't upholding the 1986 moratorium. Not the robust action we were hoping for, but better than going backward. And it all happened because we got people to talk and think about animals in

Me, then-Los Angeles Mayor Eric Garcetti, Simone Reyes, Sagen Elizabeth, and Russell Simmons.

ways they hadn't before. Otherwise, that proposal would have been signed off on by the US without anyone speaking for the whales.

Little by little, we were bringing the voiceless into more conversations.

Now in 2016, because of my recommendation, a presidential candidate from a major political party had added not just animals but *animal rights* to her website.

Watching our political movement find its way into the mainstream, where it belongs, has been a dream come true.

A few weeks after the Clinton fundraiser, Simone sent me an article about a story Hillary told during a Facebook Live event with Ellen DeGeneres. She said a naturalist in Kenya told her that a herd of elephants used to come every evening to drink from a pond near his home. One night, when he was hosting a cocktail party on his veranda, the matriarch from the herd walked right up to the party, looked at all the guests, and wrapped her trunk around the arm of a woman who was wearing an ivory bracelet. In his telling, the elephant looked at the bracelet and looked at the woman, then turned and walked away. The naturalist was convinced the elephant knew where the bracelet came from.

So were we.

Backstage at the Hillary Clinton fundraiser, talking animals and presidential platforms. It seemed like a dream when candidate Clinton told us she would put an issues page about animals on her website. Never in my wildest dreams did I imagine she'd go so far as to talk about animal rights!
Left to right, Simone Reyes, me, Secretary Clinton, Sagen Elizabeth, and Lucy McIntosh.

Like everyone around me, I assumed Secretary Clinton would be the next president, so her willingness to talk about animal rights gave us immense hope. Attitudes were shifting; there was no doubt. A Gallup survey conducted in 2015 showed that almost a third of Americans believed animals should have the same rights as humans, up from 25 percent when I founded SCIL. More people than ever before said it was wrong to use animals in circuses, for sport, in lab research. These were all issues SCIL would tackle over the following years. But in 2016, we thought the next president, using one of the biggest platforms in the world, would bring animal rights straight into the heart of the national conversation.

We almost fell out of our chairs when we saw the "Protecting Animals and Wildlife" section go up on her issues page, leading with: "The way our society treats animals is a reflection of our humanity." It was more than we had even dared hope for.

CHAPTER 7

WINS IN SACRAMENTO AND BEYOND

On the legislative front, we had two big projects in 2016. The first was to get the Assembly to adopt House Resolution 28, which SCIL sponsored. California's Education Code already included provisions calling for humane education in the public school system, but the principles of respect and kindness toward animals, including wildlife, were rarely included in curricula. Our aim with HR 28 was to get the Superintendent of Public Instruction, the State Board of Education, and the California Department of Education to ensure compliance with those provisions.

Unlike bills, resolutions don't get written into law. They simply express the opinion of whatever chamber they're adopted by, potentially allowing that chamber's rules to be amended or for new committees to be created. HR 28 was introduced in 2015 by Assemblymember Matt Dababneh. By the time it came up for a vote and was adopted in May of 2016, seventy-three members from both sides of the aisle had signed on as coauthors.

It's hard to overstate how exciting it was to know that almost every assemblymember in office that year agreed that schools needed to do more to teach compassion toward animals. They understood the link between abuse and neglect of animals and violence toward humans. Our goal was to break that link as early as possible, and this law would help.

Part of our job is also to educate lawmakers.

In my very early days as a legislative advocate, I was intimidated by elected officials. It was rooted in a feeling of inadequacy about my own education level. As you might have guessed by now, I'm a bit of a rebel. That didn't go over so well with my teachers in high school. By the time I was fifteen, I was ditching regularly. We'd moved from St. Louis to the Missouri countryside at the start of my sophomore year, and it was a pretty traumatic experience for me. The new kid from the city was the favorite target of all the school bullies. Getting jumped and beaten up by three girls in the bathroom shortly after arriving convinced me that I'd never adapt to this new culture. I started spending as much time as I could with a group of older friends I'd made who were already out of school. This was the only place I felt like I fit in. When I did show up in class, it was with an attitude of defiance. My behavior at home wasn't much better. I was so far out of my element and unhappy that my family couldn't ignore it.

Eventually, my parents were called in to discuss my absences. State law said you had to be sixteen to leave school—I was a few months shy of that—but the principal was willing to make an exception in my case if they wanted to pull me out right away. They took him up on his offer.

SCIL's House Resolution 28 was meant to bring the principles of kindness and respect for animals and observance of laws, regulations, and policies pertaining to the humane treatment of animals, including wildlife, into more California classrooms. Pictured are Jane Velez-Mitchell, Katie Cleary, Simone Reyes, me, and Assemblymember Matt Dababneh.

The ride home was silent. Eventually, my mother informed me that since I wasn't in school anymore, I'd need to get a job. She let me help out in her women's clothing boutique in Ste. Genevieve,

Missouri, while I looked for something else. A few years later, I'd get my GED, and a few years after that, an associate of applied science degree in data processing, allowing me to start a successful career in information technology. But my atypical education pathway made me feel less than. The people I was dealing with in city halls and Sacramento were more polished than me and had more formal education. For a long time, I assumed that meant they were also smarter than me.

I no longer feel that way.

During the spay and neuter bill battle, I spent an hour with one lawmaker, explaining the toll the overpopulation crisis was taking on veterinarians and shelter workers, and how having to euthanize all those healthy animals was causing high turnover rates and immense suffering. When I was done, he said, "Well then, those folks ought to get into a different line of work." Just like that!

Since he had no compassion for the animals and the people who work with them, surely, I thought, I could win him over by talking about the millions of taxpayer dollars that were being wasted.

Still didn't get through.

In theory, it was his job as a legislator to care about these things and look for real solutions to real problems. I'd learned to keep my cool and be diplomatic no matter what, but in situations like this, with such total heartlessness on display, I admit it was tough.

Only one lawmaker has ever caused me to lose my temper. It was in 2017, when SCIL was working to kick puppy mills out of California pet stores. A Democratic assemblymember sat attentively as I explained exactly how horrific conditions are for animals in those mills, how they're treated like inanimate objects, and then tossed out like trash. He bobbed his head as he listened and seemed to be really getting what I was saying. When I was done, he came out with the most insane proposal I could have imagined. "California should have its own puppy mills! It'd be a great money-maker for the state, and we could regulate the industry."

After everything he'd just heard, this was his solution!

I just didn't have the patience to deal with such nonsense that day. My lead lobbyist on the bill was running late and had missed the first part of the meeting. She was hurrying toward the room when she heard me start yelling. What a relief when she arrived! I let her conduct the rest of the meeting while I calmed down in the hallway. It wasn't worth wasting my breath anyway. Some people cannot be reached.

Also making its way through the legislature in 2016, with sponsoring support from SCIL, was Senate Bill 1200, which focused on animal cruelty and criminal statistics. Our goal was to add yet another layer of education in society, this time within law enforcement. As adopted, the bill required that probation officers receive specific training on domestic violence including, but not limited to, the nexus between animal cruelty and violence against persons. It also ordered the California Department of Justice to include in its annual report to the governor information regarding arrests for animal cruelty. SB 1200 made it through both houses without a single no vote and was signed into law in August by Governor Jerry Brown.

Small steps are huge milestones when it comes to animal cruelty laws. We work on this issue constantly.

In 2023, Assembly Bill 829, the Animal Cruelty and Violence Intervention Act, authored by Assemblymember Marie Waldron and sponsored by SCIL, was signed into law by Governor Gavin Newsom. It expands counseling requirements for those convicted of animal abuse crimes and encourages judges to order mental health evaluations that can potentially lead to more extensive treatment than the counseling currently required. It would have been difficult to pass without being able to quantify, thanks to SB 1200, the number of people who were being arrested for animal abuse crimes that justified more extensive psychological assessments.

■ ■ ■

After the successful passage of SB 1200, we normally would have spent the last few months of the year tying up loose ends and getting ready for the next legislative session. I often had too many irons in the fire to take real time off during the holidays, but the week after Thanksgiving was usually fairly quiet for SCIL.

Not in 2016.

On November 28, the Monday after Thanksgiving, I got a call informing me that the California Department of Fish and Wildlife (CDFW) had just issued a permit for a landowner to kill beloved mountain lion P-45, the "King of Malibu."

P-45 was part of an ongoing mountain lion study launched by the National Park Services in the Santa Monica Mountains in 2002. Study cats are identified with a P for puma, followed by the number indicating where they fit in the study. He was the forty-fifth cat added. Of course every mountain lion is critical in the fight to protect the species, but this one had a special place in the hearts of wildlife lovers. Biological samples taken in 2015 showed that he was born in a different region and had safely traveled across the busiest freeways in Los Angeles to enter this new territory. That was a miracle on its own. He brought with him new genes that conservationists hoped could save a local population otherwise facing local extinction due to its isolation and lack of genetic diversity.

Soon after moving into his new range, P-45 mated with P-19, producing at least two kittens in November of 2015. This is the kind of development conservationists dream of. Researchers had been predicting that the species could disappear from the area within fifty years. The arrival of this new breeding-age male had the potential to change everything. Hope was in the air.

Now CDFW had put a hit out on P-45.

The story is as exasperating as they come. With the passage in 1990 of Proposition 117, the California Wildlife Protection Act, mountain lions gained "specially protected mountain species" status and could be legally hunted only if they were found to be harming life, livestock, or property. So when a rancher complained that ten of her alpacas had been killed by a mountain lion over the weekend, CDFW said it was obligated to issue a ten-day depredation permit authorizing the rancher to kill the animal she believed to be the culprit.

We needed to organize quickly.

I was informed that on the Wednesday after Thanksgiving—forty-eight hours after the ten-day depredation permit was issued—CDFW was holding a general workshop with the theme "Living with Mountain Lions" in Agoura Hills, near the Santa Monica Mountains P-45 called home.

Right away, I sent out an email telling supporters that P-45 had a target on his back and that it was up to us to save him. We had to flood CDFW's offices with calls and emails and attend the Agoura Hills meeting. I reached out to every local elected official within P-45's range, letting them know what was happening in their backyard. Many had already heard the news and made plans to attend. Assemblymember Richard Bloom, Senators Ben Allen and Henry Stern, and LA County Supervisor Sheila Kuehl were all scheduled to be there. My plan was to hold a press conference in the room the workshop would be in, right before it started.

Though his district wasn't within P-45's range, LA City Councilmember Paul Koretz, an animal lover through and through, promised to join us.

Agoura Hills is normally an eighty-minute drive from my house when the roads are clear. But there's no such thing as a traffic-free weekday in Southern California. I set out three hours before the scheduled start time and hoped for the best.

About halfway into the drive, the calls started coming in. "Judie, the news outlets are all here. They're lined up around the block. You've got to get here!"

Did I mention that I'd sent out the notice to my media list? Of course I did. This story wasn't about ranchers' property rights, and we weren't going to let CDFW frame it that way. It was about respecting the natural predators that were here long before any of us.

Animals that don't have owners have rights too.

After what felt like the longest drive of my life, I pulled into the parking lot and, to my astonishment, saw a long line of TV trucks near the building with their satellite dishes all set up. My first thought was that CDFW was going to accuse us of hijacking their event. That concern quickly gave way to excitement. P-45 was a rock star and deserved all this attention.

I pulled into what was definitely not an official parking space and ran straight inside. The SCIL crew stood on one side of the podium, which had a dozen microphones on it, ready to speak after me. The room was packed so full that people were lined up around the perimeter. It was standing room only! In front of the podium, supporters had placed a cardboard cutout of P-45.

The team urgently motioned me up to the microphone.

The press conference we put together right before the CDFW workshop was a success. The P-45 cutout in front of the podium helped us remind everyone how magnificent mountain lions are.

About an hour into the drive, I'd undone the top button on my pants for breathing room for the long drive ahead, and in my haste, I totally forgot to button it again. Luckily, I was behind the podium, and wearing a long jacket when I remembered.

Still catching my breath, I began to tell the crowd the story from P-45's point of view. How someone had imported these alpacas from South America and left them out overnight in enclosures that weren't lion-proof, in the middle of mountain lion country, then complained when P-45 did what he was hard-wired to do.

By this point, the rancher had started backtracking, saying her intention wasn't to kill P-45, just to have him relocated. Really? Now she wanted to put him at risk by shipping him off to a territory he didn't know, and threaten the population he was leaving behind with local extinction just because she didn't have proper pens for her animals? Did she think no other mountain lions would ever come onto her property?

Close to three hundred people showed up that night—way more than anyone was expecting, especially CDFW. Some were there because they had livestock and genuine questions about how to protect them. Most came to be P-45's voice. Representatives from Project Bobcat, Project Coyote, and the Mountain Lion Foundation, including Leah Sturgis, who would join the SCIL board two years later, all spoke. A Park Service biologist presented satellite data showing that P-45 generally stayed away from humans and ranches. Since the study was launched, there had never been an attack on people.

CDFW officials were not pleased. The quiet workshop they'd planned with the best of intentions had turned into a high-profile event with local and national TV stations there to put the spotlight on a bad decision the department had made.

The meeting ended with photos of P-45's cubs up on a screen, and the mountain lion activists cheering. By that time, the landowner, under pressure from a variety of groups, including the county supervisor, had agreed to work with us and wildlife authorities to find other ways to keep her alpacas safe. We organized a conference call with her and other parties the next day and convinced her to let Mountain Lion Foundation erect four lion-proof pens, donated by a wildlife group, on her property. These are inexpensive structures that can be built in just a few hours with a small crew and usually don't even require a permit. The design can be tailored to the specific types of pets or livestock on the property and the type of predator they're being protected from.

Thus a simple, economical solution was found to a problem CDFW was ready to address by issuing a depredation permit. The alpacas were happy in their pens, and the mountain lions understood that they were off-limits. Everybody won. P-45 lived to see another day.

I shudder to think what the outcome could have been without the public pressure on CDFW officers and that landowner. What if we hadn't all showed up to speak for the voiceless mountain lions?

I was informed later that CDFW officials were furious that we'd staged a "guerrilla" press conference and hijacked their workshop. Whatever. It worked. Clips from our press conference were everywhere. One ended up on *Good Morning America*—that's how viral the thing was. All the next day, I got one Google alert after another as press coverage widened. "Mountain lion known as P-45 no longer faces the death penalty," announced the *LA Times*. An article in the *New York Times* asked, "Big cat attacks alpacas. Does he deserve to die?"

For a little while at least, P-45 was safe, and more people than ever were cognizant of the threats facing mountain lions in some parts of California.

Encouragingly, the mountain lion study has grown to 121 cats, not counting kittens. Each has its own "Puma Profile" on the National Park Service website.

Sadly, P-45's profile mentions that his status is uncertain. His radio-collar hasn't transmitted since February 2018, and efforts to locate him have been unsuccessful. There's been no sign of him on any of the numerous trail cameras within his range. Those who follow the population closely assume he's dead. Researchers conducting the study estimate that he was probably born in 2012 or 2013, so he would have been five or six.

Not a long life for a big cat in the wild, but it could have ended in 2016 if we all hadn't showed up for him that night.

CHAPTER 8

THE REAL COST OF THAT DOGGY IN THE WINDOW

When I started saying I was going to kick puppy mills out of California pet shops, only a handful of people believed me. Dr. Gary Michelson and SCIL board members knew I meant it. But other animal rights groups said it was impossible. Maybe in a few years, they said. Several of them planned to tackle the issue later, when *they* were ready.

Well, *I* was ready in 2017.

What I'd experienced on the ground in New Orleans after Katrina, and on the shelter tour I did across California during the spay and neuter bill, still haunted me, all these years later. And we still hadn't made any substantial progress in reducing the number of animals entering and dying in our shelters.

Besides a spay and neuter bill (you know how that ended) and mandatory microchipping (which we finally got done in 2020), I knew we needed to stop the steady flow of mill-bred animals into

California through pet stores. Because while our shelters were euthanizing all those healthy, adoptable dogs, cats, and rabbits every year, pet stores were continuously filling their cages with animals purchased from high-volume mills, mostly in the Midwest.

Puppy mills were the biggest actors in this space, and the most high-profile offenders, because demand for designer dogs was the main engine keeping the industry going. But cats and rabbits were being bred and killed in the same sickening conditions, and I was determined to shut that down too.

Mill operators need compelling lies to keep their profit machines running. Pet stores that sell mill-bred animals are perfect accomplices, partners in crime if you will, since they too make money off breeders' negligent and cruel practices.

Customers are told they're purchasing animals with documented health histories and "guarantees." They're led to believe that purebreds will exhibit specific personality traits and temperaments. Sadly, all this smoke and mirrors works on unsuspecting buyers. Those so-called guarantees are mostly meaningless and often have more exclusions than inclusions. Veterinarians have stories galore about puppy mill dogs being brought to them with severe health problems. Many are born into squalor and ripped away from their mothers at just a few weeks old, to be packed into a truck and shipped off to a pet store in a different state. The puppies transported to California might spend a whole day in the back of an eighteen-wheeler with no food or water, confined in a tiny cage for the entire journey with no wellness checks along the way.

It's not uncommon for the puppies to die en route. Their bodies simply get dumped at the destination.

Accidents occur as well. In 2006, an eighteen-wheeler delivering puppies from the Hunte Corporation caught fire after a thousand-mile trip. The sixty puppies inside were burned alive. Fines were paid and deliveries resumed as usual. Just the cost of doing business for a big commercial breeder.

All these lies meant families were being lured into buying puppies that were "certified" when they could have been adopting healthy and happy shelter animals. If they really had their heart set on a certain kind of dog, they could go to one of the countless breed-specific rescues operating in the state or look online at sites such as Petfinder.com and Adoptapet.com, which aggregate animals from thousands of shelters and rescue groups. It's never been easier to adopt a specific kind of dog, if that's your thing. A woman I know has been running the same German Shepherd rescue for over twenty-five years and has adopted out over 10,000 dogs. Like other conscientious rescue groups, she does thorough checks to make sure the adopting family is a good fit, reducing the chances of the animal being returned to the group or relinquished to a shelter.

Meanwhile, people continue to buy mill-bred German Shepherds only to get them home and discover that they have all manner of congenital diseases and behavioral problems.

These dogs often wind up in shelters, or worse, dumped by the side of a road, thrown over a fence, or abandoned in some other disgusting way. And the cycle continues.

Another part of the mill propaganda machine is the idea that these puppies come from licensed breeders. According to federal law, businesses that use animals, including zoos, research institutions, and commercial breeders, must be licensed by the US Department of Agriculture (USDA). Sounds reassuring, doesn't it? Surely if a facility passes an inspection by a federal agency, conditions there must be decent, right?

Wrong.

This licensing sham is a perfect example of how exploiters get away with murder while decent people are tricked into supporting an indecent industry.

Breeders get licensed through the USDA's Animal Care Program, operated under its Animal and Plant Health Inspection Services, or APHIS. In theory, inspectors make unannounced visits to puppy mills and the other facilities they are supposed to regulate to document violations of the Animal Welfare Act (AWA) and take action against offenders. Any facility that has more than four "breeding females" (it pains me to adopt that terminology to talk about these poor sweet animals, but that is what the law calls them), or sells puppies wholesale or sight unseen to pet stores, brokers, or online, must be federally licensed.

In 2017, when we started working on the puppy mill bill, APHIS had an estimated 120 inspectors monitoring all licensed breeders, research facilities using animals, distributors, and other related businesses in the United States. These same 120 people were also responsible for enforcing regulations regarding GMO crops and livestock breeding.

How could such a small number of people be expected to cover that much ground, conduct meaningful inspections, and write useful reports on everything they found? They couldn't. Not with some 2,000 federally licensed dog breeders and countless other animal businesses across the country.

The standards breeders have to meet couldn't be lower. Written in 1966, the AWA set out the absolute bare minimum breeders must do to keep their license in good standing. Cages only need to be a few inches bigger than the animals inside them. It's legal to leave the dogs in these cramped spaces for their entire lives, with no contact at all with other dogs or even people. They can be given just enough food and water to stay alive. In many cases, they don't get even one hour of exercise, never touching grass or anything soft in their lives. Females are kept pregnant continuously, their bodies never given a chance to recover between litters. Once they're bred out, the females are often killed and their bodies dumped. Cages are left outside, day and night, in scorching heat and brutal cold. The cages are rarely cleaned, so the dogs sit and sleep in their own excrement. These are *licensed* facilities we're talking about. Every one of these practices is permitted under the AWA. Even the USDA recognizes that AWA standards are lacking, and encourages breeders to exceed them, though it can't force them to do so. Local laws can fill in some gaps, but often provide few additional protections for animals and even less enforcement.

In 2003, four years before it spent massively to defeat our spay and neuter bill in California, the Missouri-based Hunte Corporation, the biggest puppy mill operator in the country (since rebranded to "Choice Puppies") and known to the animal welfare community as the worst, was cited by the Missouri Department of Natural Resources for burying more than a thousand pounds of dead puppies per acre per year on their property. You read that right. Missouri law allows breeders to bury *up to a thousand pounds of animal bodies per acre* on their land every year. Why only a thousand pounds? Because beyond that limit, there's a risk of environmental hazard. Nothing to do with ethical concerns. It doesn't matter how the animals are killed, either. Or why. Females may be bred out. Maybe puppies don't meet specific designer criteria. "Imperfect" ones get tossed out like dirty rags. Sick dogs get killed and buried to avoid paying for veterinary care.

Sometimes diseases run rampant through the facilities and the breeders slaughter all the puppies and start over.

Every one of these actions is allowed under the AWA. And the AWA is the only law that governs the operations of federally licensed breeders.

There's no limit on how many puppies these facilities can produce. Estimates vary, but it's safe to assume that all facilities, licensed and unlicensed combined, churn out more than two million dogs a year. Way more than will ever be placed in homes, especially with millions of shelter animals waiting to be adopted.

Word was getting out about how deeply disgusting and disturbing the practices of puppy mills were, but big breeders were countering with ads depicting their facilities as beautiful places with blue skies in the background and happy and healthy puppies bounding joyfully across lush green lawns. Absolute propaganda and totally deceptive, but people were buying it. And buying the designer puppies.

Education and outreach were not doing the trick. Only a change in the law would change behavior, and thus bring down demand.

■ ■ ■

Back when I was working on the spay and neuter bill, California State Veterinarian Dr. Ben Sun invited me to his office to give me some perspective on how dire the mill problem was. State law required that a health certificate be sent to his office for every puppy put up for sale in the state, in theory so that buyers could see the origin of the animal they were purchasing. Dr. Sun led me into a cubicle piled to the ceiling with white file boxes, each filled with nothing but health certificates from puppy mills, mostly the biggest and most ruthless mill operators in the country. The same ones that were doing everything in their power to defeat our bill. My jaw dropped. No wonder the overpopulation problem was so massive and just getting worse. I asked how many years' worth of certificates those boxes contained. One year, he said. I couldn't believe my ears. We counted the certificates in one box and multiplied by the number of boxes and came to a total of 85,000.

California had no control over how these out-of-state mills operated. Pet stores didn't have to disclose much about the animals they sold, just their age, breed, and where they came from. If you went into any pet shop in the state, the company names displayed on the cages told the whole story. All puppy factories. Not a single responsible breeder. Why? Because responsible breeders would never sell to pet shops. They want to know exactly where their animals are going. Commercial breeders just want to move the merchandise. Get the puppies out the door so they can churn out more like any other commodity.

California's ranking as the world's fifth-largest economy gives it enormous influence. There's truth to the saying that as California goes, so goes the nation. When our state makes changes, other states watch. SCIL is very mindful of that economic power. Others were likely to follow our lead if we kicked puppy mills out of pet stores.

Now our task was to tell lawmakers a story they would understand about how the new law would be good for animals, good for pet owners, good for business, and good for California taxpayers, since more people would adopt from shelters.

SCIL had sponsored legislation to crack down on puppy mills before. Authored by Assemblymember Pedro Nava and introduced in February of 2009, Assembly Bill 241, the Responsible Breeder Act, would have limited to fifty the number of unsterilized dogs and cats an individual or business could have on their property. Breeders that got caught breaking the law would have to either re-home the excess animals or have them sterilized.

Let's be clear: we're talking about a very low bar. No ethical breeder would have anywhere near fifty animals at one time. I wanted the number to be much lower, but our lobbyist convinced me it was the only way to get it done. Fifty would look reasonable to legislators. Being forced to rehome some animals or have them fixed wasn't much of a penalty either.

Nonetheless, all the usual bad actors jumped right in to fight the bill. The American Kennel Club (AKC), in particular, threw around the insane idea that as long as animals were getting quality care in these mills, it didn't matter how many of them there were. Never mind that the AKC did its registrations mainly through the mail, without visiting facilities. It couldn't possibly say one way or the other how these animals were being raised and treated.

AB 241 passed both houses but was vetoed by Governor Arnold Schwarzenegger, who ended up buying into the nonsense about the fifty-animal cap being arbitrary and the bill jeopardizing the businesses of those who raised service and assistance dogs.

We worked hard to get that bill through and were devastated when it was shot down. California had been so good about breaking new ground when it came to animal rights, but on this issue, here we were falling behind!

It was all the more painful because a second iteration of our spay and neuter bill also died in committee that same year, 2009, again due to the misinformation machine working overtime.

■ ■ ■

Laguna Beach had been my home for almost twenty years when I brought SCIL's proposal to ban retail sales of animals from commercial breeders to the city council in early 2012. Several neighboring cities had similar ordinances. An animal control officer let me know that pet store operators were constantly inquiring about setting up shop in Laguna, something she discouraged them from doing. There were no stores selling mill-bred animals within the city limits when I started, and I intended to keep it that way. Up the road in Newport Beach, animal rights activists I knew were protesting regularly outside a pet store that sold mill animals. I appreciated the activists' time and effort, but I knew the needle wasn't moving.

When the Laguna Beach ban was first discussed by the city council in March of 2012, people crowded into the chamber to express their support. Council directed staff to draft an ordinance, which was approved two months later, in May. Dr. Matthew Wheaton, a local veterinarian, gave incredibly powerful testimony about how thousands of mill-bred animals were brought to his practice soon after being purchased, presenting one or more diseases directly related to conditions in the mills. He was certain that if people knew about those conditions, they would refuse to buy those animals. The room was silent after he spoke.

The ordinance was adopted on May 1.

Next stop: the city of Los Angeles, where I got my start in legislative advocacy. The seven municipal shelters LA operated were overrun with animals purchased from pet stores then relinquished to city facilities. LA city and county shelters were euthanizing more than 70,000 animals a year. All at taxpayer expense.

Just as California paves the way for other states in many areas, when it comes to protecting animal rights, Los Angeles often shows other large cities how things are done. City Councilmember Paul Koretz, with whom I had worked on a number of animal issues and ordinances, introduced a motion in May 2011, summing the problem up in these words: "By being customers, we perpetuate the problem."

In addition to stopping sales of mill-bred animals in pet stores, the motion asked for a study on banning mills operating inside the city. We had no idea how many of those there were. Some were completely off the grid, breeding animals in warehouses in the most disgusting conditions you can imagine, then selling them on the street for next to nothing. A bona fide cash crop for these heartless people. Demand was high, too, since the animals were so cheap. This was before classified ad websites became popular, so breeders would advertise in local newspapers or post signs on telephone poles.

Needless to say, the animals were often sick and ended up getting taken straight to shelters. And the cycle continued.

We won an early motion to prohibit pet stores from selling mill-bred dogs, cats, chickens, and rabbits and ban the establishment or operation of mills within city limits in April 2012. The next step was passing an ordinance to make the policy official.

We had to deal with the usual scare tactics about how this change would put all sorts of small pet stores out of business and literally mean the end of dogs and cats in Los Angeles. The exploiters never gave up! Over and over again, they forced us to spend too much of our time countering their lies. It's by far one of the most exhausting aspects of this work. They're always hoping we'll just give up and walk away.

They don't know us.

In this instance, the support was overwhelming, and drowned out the whining of the special interests. Residents were outraged that Los Angeles was a source of profits for puppy mill operators. Even the *LA Times* editorial board came out in favor of the ordinance, citing the horrific conditions documented in puppy mills and the near total lack of oversight and enforcement. In its editorial dated August 5, 2012, the board mentioned a 2010 audit conducted by the USDA's Office of Inspector General, which found that the agency's animal care inspectors "failed to sanction appropriately, or quickly, breeders holding dogs variously infested with ticks or sores, suffering injured limbs, living in fetid cages, unsheltered from cold or hot weather, or using water and food dishes covered in vermin. During the three-year period of the audit, USDA officials made 8,289 inspections and found that 5,261 licensed dealers were in violation of the Act."

Absolutely scathing.

The audit also noted that any effort to tighten up rules governing breeding mills would face massive opposition from the pet industry and breeding businesses along with their legislative allies. I could confirm that.

The graphic description of what goes on in puppy mills, and clear language about who opposes tougher laws and why, further helped our cause.

On October 31, 2012, the LA City Council approved the new ordinance on a 13-to-2 vote. Los Angeles thus became the largest American city to enact legislation to stop the flow of mill-bred animals into its community via pet shops. Because city officials were nervous about the move, and to put to rest all the fearmongering by opponents, I suggested that they add a three-year sunset clause. In other words, create a trial period to show that the ordinance wouldn't cause the sky to fall, as our opponents claimed it would.

The ordinance took effect mid-2013 with massive public support.

The sky did not fall. In fact, the pet stores that connected shelter and rescued animals with new owners thrived.

Seeing nothing but positive results, when the moratorium ended in April 2016, the city council voted to permanently ban mill-bred dogs, cats, and rabbits from pet stores, retail businesses, and other commercial establishments within the city of Los Angeles.

Celebrating the City of LA's adoption of a puppy mill ban with Maggie Q and City Councilmember Paul Koretz.

Euthanasia rates decreased. The city was on the right track. As City Councilmember Koretz put it, LA had made considerable progress in three years in "choking off that supply line."

SCIL was the driving force behind this change. Clearly the time had come for us to take the fight to Sacramento again. The wind was in our sails.

We were ready to get a really big thing done.

CHAPTER 9

FIGHTING THE OPPOSITION—AND ALLIES

Before winning a seat in the California State Assembly, Patrick O'Donnell earned a reputation as a defender of animal welfare on the Long Beach City Council. His involvement in animal issues in his hometown had given him a clear picture of the horrific situation in shelters and rescues, and the burden it placed on the resources of local governments.

He also knew about the abuse and trauma animals suffer in breeding mills.

Judy Crumpton was herself a major voice for animals in Long Beach, where she had acted as our city coordinator for the spay and neuter bill. A big supporter of SCIL's work, Judy knew about my dream of getting mill-bred animals out of pet shops across the state, and what a huge mountain it would be to climb.

After Patrick O'Donnell was elected to the Assembly, Judy asked if I had considered talking to him about carrying that puppy mill bill that had been in a holding pattern for years.

At the time, most lawmakers were still shying away from vanguard legislation having to do with animal rights. These bills were seen as lightning rods. Too noisy. Not worth the hassle. Definitely not worth losing the contributions they got from animal industries that had a lot of sway in the legislature.

It takes a special kind of courage to move forward despite all this pressure. Sadly, that courage is not something you find in many politicians. Too many of them let the power and money go to their heads as soon as they get elected. They love feeling important and don't ever want to go back to being regular citizens and riding in the elevator with the little people. Staying in power becomes their top priority. The constituents they're supposed to serve are an afterthought, a group they only care about when the next election comes around. They can rationalize all they want, say they need to do certain things to stay in office so they can keep doing good work, but in the end, for these lawmakers, it's all about staying in power.

I've known a few legislators who don't back down in the face of adversity. Assemblymember O'Donnell was one of them.

When I first went to his Sacramento office with my lobbyist to pitch the puppy mill bill to him and his staff, they actually seemed excited. They knew it would be a heavy lift but were invested in the issue and ready to take on the fight.

Obviously, they didn't know what they were getting into. They found out soon enough. The day after they agreed to help us, the opposition machine went into high gear.

Assembly Bill 485, the Pet Rescue and Adoption Act, authored by Patrick O'Donnell with Matt Dababneh as the principal coauthor

Our kickoff press conference at the State Capitol. Pictured from left to right are Amitis Ariano, Simone Reyes, Assemblymember Patrick O'Donnell, Henry Brzezinski, me, Katie Cleary, Assemblymember Matt Dababneh, Dr. Karen Halligan, and Andrew Kim.

and sponsored by SCIL, was introduced in February 2017. As submitted, the landmark bill would make it illegal for pet store operators to sell live dogs, cats, or rabbits obtained from high-volume commercial breeding farms. Instead, pet shops could offer for adoption animals from public animal control agencies or shelters, or from contracted shelters and rescues. Shelter animals were, after all, the official state pet, thanks to SCIL. It was time to build on that success by getting more animals out of shelters and rescues and into loving homes.

AB 485 was referred to its first committee, Business and Professions, in March. Shortly thereafter, Assemblymember O'Donnell asked me to meet him in a small coffee shop in Huntington Beach to get the lowdown on the people springing up out of nowhere to oppose the bill. By this time, I knew all the players and their playbook by heart. For the most part, it was the same groups that had fought the spay and neuter bill, with a few new and surprising faces joining the line-up.

The American Kennel Club (AKC) came out swinging. Naturally. Remember, these are the folks who make money issuing certification papers to breeders. Of course, these papers mostly mean that paperwork was filed and fees were paid. No guarantee that the dog isn't the product of extreme inbreeding and overbreeding and won't have severe health problems as a consequence.

Starting in April, the AKC turned on the misinformation firehose full blast. Labeling those of us who supported the bill crazy anti-breeder extremists whose ultimate goal was to ban all animal ownership. Reviving the "pet extinction" propaganda from the 2007 playbook. Making it sound like getting an animal from a shelter or rescue was dicey in terms of temperament. They compared shelter animals to prisoners in jail, implying that they were somehow "broken," while dogs from breeders were not. They claimed rescues were likelier to wind up back in shelters because of behavioral issues when the opposite was true. Mill-bred animals also had a greater likelihood of being dumped in shelters with diseases that required serious veterinary care. Any vet could confirm this.

These groups insisted that shelters and rescues were "unregulated and uninspected sources," whereas commercial breeders had the stamp of approval of the USDA (as we know, that stamp is perfectly worthless).

A host of other special interests, allied directly or indirectly with breeders, jumped on the opposition bandwagon. Some were huge groups with major industry-backed resources, including the Animal

Council and NAIA. One look at the names on the boards of those organizations told us why they were siding with breeders and exploiters.

The Pet Industry Joint Advisory Council and California Retailers Association were spreading lies about how the bill would be bad for pet shops. It was their job to make sure no new restrictions were placed on them, no matter how much harm their business models were causing. Like clockwork, they spouted their same old talking points about the regulations being unreasonable and how consumers had the right to buy any kind of animal they wanted from anyone they wanted to buy from.

Animal rights was not their concern.

The breeders themselves were there, of course—the Hunte Corporation, Landauer—alongside pet store chain Petland, putting a new face on the same old drivel from the spay and neuter bill fight. They dispatched people to Assemblymember O'Donnell's office to say, "Hey, I own a pet store and I could go out of business and it will be your fault!" We researched all these people and of course there wasn't a pet store owner in the lot. None of them were who they said they were. Most were dog breeders from the Midwest, sent to pose as pet store owners and try to convince lawmakers the economy would grind to a halt if this bill passed.

Much more surprising to me were the challenges from organizations that should in theory have been behind us. Some of the biggest animal welfare groups in the country came out immediately against the bill. They claimed to want to do away with puppy mills as much as we did, but the time wasn't right. Why couldn't we hold off for another year? The truth is they wanted their name on the bill, and that couldn't happen if we kept moving forward. The train was leaving the station, and they weren't on it.

The top state advocate for one of these organizations marched into Assemblymember O'Donnell's office right after he introduced the bill, in a frantic state. "You need to pull this bill now!" she yelled. "You'll do the cause more harm than good!"

I couldn't believe it when Assemblymember O'Donnell told me about this. What was she even talking about? Thirty-six local jurisdictions in California had banned sales of mill-bred animals in local retail pet stores. Having a statewide policy would make it infinitely easier for regulators to track compliance and for business owners to comply. It made sense from the perspective of government and business. Public opinion was with us. The political winds were in our sails. I could feel it in my gut.

No matter what those other groups said, our timing could not have been better. Yet here they were, working overtime to tank the bill!

A few months later, when they saw the writing on the wall, that we had momentum and were going to succeed, suddenly these groups were in our camp—and even claiming to be the driving force behind the bill. One after the other, they put out press releases boasting about how they "Got it done!" They gave quotes to reporters suggesting that they had played a central role in the fight and even spearheaded it.

The old adage is true. Failure is an orphan, but success has many fathers.

I do what I do for the animals. Not for the recognition. When other groups do amazing things, I acknowledge and applaud them. We should all be on the same team. Watching all these so-called allies take credit for a success they had tried to undermine was painful. It was especially galling because some of them were sitting on hundreds of millions of dollars that were going to high salaries for top executives and glitzy fundraising campaigns, while we worked day and night to scrape together the money to get this bill over the finish line.

I later found out that toward the end of 2017, a few of these groups were cold-calling my major donors to try to divert money away from SCIL and into their fat war chests. It felt like I was running a marathon, going the distance, eyes on the finish line, only to have some should-be allies throwing rocks at me from the sidelines.

The puppy mill issue had taken on even more urgency after Donald Trump's election.

On February 3, 2017, two weeks after his inauguration and ten days before AB 485 was introduced, the new president had allowed the USDA to purge documents detailing animal abuse from its website. For over a decade, those monitoring animal rights could go to the site for information about people and companies violating the Horse Protection Act and Animal Welfare Act, including dog breeders. With this purge, even an ethical pet store owner who didn't want to buy from an unethical puppy mill had no way of checking on its sources' practices. Some of the documents were reposted a few weeks later, but heavily redacted. Others could only be obtained through Freedom of Information Act requests that could take years to be fulfilled. It was all part of Trump's broader push to deregulate industries and remove protections for people and animals.

We were horrified; the bad actors were thrilled. Trump's agriculture secretary had close ties to the puppy mill industry, and that only added another layer of conflict.

It took three full years, until February 2020, for the USDA to repost the full inspection reports to its website, along with new ones generated during that three-year interim. Its motivation? Congress had passed a spending bill that ordered it to make all the records available in a searchable database. Otherwise, all that history might have been lost.

As AB 485, the Pet Rescue and Adoption Act, wound its way through the legislative process, opponents pitched amendments to allow pet stores to buy from big breeders as long as they were USDA-licensed and had not been cited for Animal Welfare Act violations in the prior two years. With the document purge, though, there was no way to track violations.

It takes quite a bit of time to explain to someone who doesn't follow these issues closely why a USDA license or inspection report is meaningless and how toothless the Animal Welfare Act is. Few will stay tuned long enough to hear the whole story. But a scrubbed website? No one questioned what that meant.

Assemblymember O'Donnell was an incredible ally. He and his staff stayed the course when the going got tough. I was worried at one point, early in the process, when the waters were starting to get choppy, that he'd jump ship. As we walked into the first committee hearing together, he looked at me and said, "Mancuso, what on earth have you gotten me into?"

I certainly couldn't blame him for having a moment of doubt. What we were going to do would not be easy.

When SCIL goes into a legislative battle, everybody has a role. Mine is that of political leader. Most of my work is done behind the scenes, courting lawmakers, managing lobbyists, and organizing public relations with celebrities and the media. I also rally the grassroots supporters who make our successes possible, and I handle the fundraising that keeps it all going.

A key challenge is to make sure the arguments presented in committee hearings are as convincing as possible. That means identifying and recruiting the best witnesses we can. My team usually coordinates with the author's staff on this phase, though sometimes we are given free rein. We spend weeks preparing those who will give testimony for us.

Committee hearings are absolutely crucial. They give legislators a chance to hear directly from the people on the frontlines of the issue a bill seeks to address. Good witnesses can make or break a campaign.

The testimony given for AB 485 could not have been more compelling.

Andrew Kim is the cofounder and CEO of Healthy Spot, a Santa Monica-based chain selling natural pet food and supplies. In 2017, when he came to testify to the Business and Professions Committee, he had over two hundred employees and eight locations, with plans to expand to more than ten within the year.

Andrew wasted no time telling the committee exactly how good the bill would be for pet stores. He credited his own success to a business model based on partnerships with local rescues and shelters. One by one, he debunked the lies our opponents were telling about the negative impacts of the law.

Assemblymember Patrick O'Donnell, me, and Los Angeles City Councilmember Paul Koretz, whose testimony reassured lawmakers that the world didn't end when LA passed its puppy mill ban.

"Despite opponents' claims to the contrary, transitioning to an adoption-based model has proven to be successful for many business owners," he explained. "Healthy Spot is not a nonprofit. I want to be clear that we are a business that believes in profits with principles. We have been thriving because of the approach we have taken and the support we have received from the community in doing so."

The purpose of the hearing was to inform committee members how AB 485 would impact business. Andrew reassured them that it was easy for pet store owners to transition to a more modern and ethical model while, as a side benefit, reducing overcrowding in shelters. Everyone comes out ahead. Stores' business models become more sustainable since they reflect the world they operate in, consumers get healthier pets and stop supporting the puppy factory industry, more adoptable animals get into loving homes, and the state of California has more resources to direct elsewhere.

It was very difficult to argue with what Andrew was saying, though our opponents gave it their best shot.

Another phenomenal ally in moving the bill through the committees was Henry Brzezinski, who at the time was the Legislative Chair of the California Animal Control Directors Association. After witnessing firsthand the tragedy unfolding in shelters over many years, Henry drew a clear line for committee members between that situation and the number of mill animals being churned out. As a humane officer, he was tasked with inspecting puppy mills when complaints were made against them. He saw the horror up close. Henry affirmed in no uncertain terms that it would *never* be possible to absorb all the animals coming out of those mills into homes, especially with so many requiring extensive medical care. In his professional opinion, AB 485's impact on businesses and consumers would be positive across the board.

Rounding out personal testimony to support the bill was Dr. Karen Halligan, then-Chief Veterinary Officer for the Lucy Pet Foundation and a member of the SCIL board of directors.

On average, close to 2,000 new bills are proposed during each legislative session. Lawmakers can get pretty jaded listening to testimony for the ones that make it into committee. But I can tell you that when Karen testified, they were holding their breath.

After reminding the committee that, as a veterinarian, she had taken an oath to protect animals and relieve their suffering, Karen described her experience working for more than twelve years as a shelter vet. How the cages were never empty. How she had to go from one row to the next, deciding which animals would die due to a lack of space. How loving, adoptable animals would lick her hand before she put them to sleep.

This is something we had tried to convey to legislators during the spay and neuter bill battle. How the overpopulation crisis took a heavy emotional toll on veterinarians and shelter professionals. Staff turnover was high because so many people just couldn't stay in this devastatingly stressful and depressing job. High turnover meant allocating more resources to train new staff, who ended up leaving after a few years, and then their replacements had to be trained. When Karen spoke about it, it was personal. She had lived the misery, felt the pain, shed the tears. She had watched taxpayer dollars get burned up by a machine that would never slow down as long as mill-bred animals kept pouring into California.

After hearing from Andrew, Henry, and Karen, it was difficult for lawmakers to vote against the bill. AB 485 sailed through the Assembly Business and Professions Committee 10-to-1 (with five not voting) in April, then passed the Senate Business, Professions and Economic Development Committee 7-1-1 in July.

As it wound its way through the legislative process over the summer, most of the naysayers rallied to our side and helped get the bill over the finish line. It passed the Senate unanimously on

Above, me testifying before the Assembly Appropriations Committee. Below, press conference celebrating the passage of AB 485. Back row: Nick Sackett, Assemblymember Matt Dababneh, and Andrew Kim. Front row: a Love & Leashes rescue partner, Katie Cleary, me, Simone Reyes, Jane Velez-Mitchell, Joanna Krupa, and Haze Lynn. Kneeling in front: a Love & Leashes rescue partner.

September 12 and made it through the concurrence vote in the Assembly two days later on a 65-to-3 vote, with eleven not voting.

Despite the best efforts of breeders and exploiters to get him to change his mind, Governor Jerry Brown signed the Pet Rescue and Adoption Act into law on October 17, 2017. It took effect on January 1, 2019.

Since then, seven other states and countless local jurisdictions have followed our lead, increasing the number of animals saved exponentially.

CHAPTER 10

BUILDING ON MOMENTUM

The popularity of the puppy mill bill did not go unnoticed by legislators. Historically, they'd had every incentive to be on the wrong side of animal issues. Now the tide had turned. Those who got behind AB 485 were feeling the love. Lawmakers who had never given me the time of day were suddenly offering to author bills for SCIL.

Because we took on the mill-bred animal issue in the right way and at the right time, we shifted what people thought was possible to achieve with legislation. Supporting animal causes had become a political winner.

By February 2018, just four months after the puppy mill bill passed, SCIL had found authors for *eight* animal bills. Unprecedented. At no time before would that many lawmakers have put their names on legislation for us or any other animal rights group. I had no idea how unusual it was to have so many irons in the fire.

People would stop me in the halls of the Capitol and say, "Wow, you guys are on a roll." It took dozens of comments like that for me to realize just how big what we were doing was. Indeed, we *were* on a roll.

Having more legislators in our camp certainly made the next phase of SCIL's growth easier. For me personally, though, the real sea change was hiring Nickolaus Sackett. Nick first heard about SCIL in 2015, when model, actress, and SCIL board member Katie Cleary and I were working to save baby elephants that were being rounded up in the wild in Zimbabwe and shipped to China, where they were delivered to zoos or wealthy "collectors." We were certain some international law or treaty was being violated, but which one? The matter required a kind of legal expertise the lawyers SCIL worked with couldn't provide.

Here's how it happened: Katie ran into a friend at a coffee shop in Los Angeles and casually asked if he knew any lawyers who could help us save some elephants. On the spot, that friend contacted someone in a big law firm, who sent out a firm-wide email to see if anyone on staff had the background and legal expertise to lend us a hand. That email was forwarded to Nick, who was working as a corporate litigation attorney in the New York offices of that firm. Importantly, he was fresh off a two-month hiatus volunteering at an elephant sanctuary in Thailand.

Nick reached out as soon as he saw the email.

I asked what he knew about CITES, the Convention on International Trade in Endangered Species of Wild Fauna and Flora. Nothing yet, but he would learn.

He started digging and got back to me later that day. Thus began a friendship and partnership that within a few years would set SCIL on a new path.

Hands-on work with wildlife changes most people, and Nick was no exception. His time in Thailand had impacted him deeply.

Before long, he was volunteering for SCIL in his spare time. He even went to give testimony when the New York version of our Dining with Dogs bill was in committee. Based on his availability and my needs, he would help with researching, writing, and proofreading. During the puppy mill bill battle, Nick timed his trips to visit his grandparents in Sacramento to coincide with hearings so he could sit in.

Loving animals is a great feeling. Giving your time to help them directly brings a whole other level of satisfaction. Passing legislation to save and protect animals is empowering and energizing in a way that's hard to describe.

Nick had the bug. He wanted a job that he found more meaningful and allowed him to live all his values, including veganism. He was ready to make a career change. I needed in-house help, but it had to be the right person.

Most of the money SCIL raised went to pay contract lobbyists. Unfortunately, that's the only way to get legislation done. I also needed lawyers to get SCIL's analyses and legal language just right. How many hours had I spent scrambling to find an attorney who had a general understanding of an issue and could be all the way up to speed within a day or two?

Nick could do all that and learn the lobbying part on the job. Importantly, he had the passion you need to defend animal rights. It's tough going every day. If you're only halfway in, you'll be all the way out in no time. I've seen it happen over and over. Nick was all the way in.

We started discussing the possibility of a full-time position early in 2017. I knew it was the right thing to do for SCIL, but that doesn't mean I didn't have a pit in my stomach. Having someone on the payroll would be life-changing in helping with the workload, but also financially. I'd been doing everything myself on the operations side up until then and allocating nearly all the money raised to lobbyists and lawyers. There was almost nothing left over.

Even if Nick became SCIL's in-house attorney and a registered lobbyist, it would take time for him to get his sea legs, and I'd have to keep paying contract lobbyists in the meantime.

All these fears weighed on me. Scaling up is a big decision, and I couldn't just walk away if it didn't work out. I had so many concrete ideas about how to help animals. What would happen to them if I ran out of money? At the same time, I was aware I'd lose the momentum from the puppy mill bill if I didn't build on it. Countless people had told me that, and I knew it in my bones. SCIL would stagnate if it didn't grow, and stagnating was not an option.

In November 2017, I offered Nick a job, and he accepted. We agreed he'd start in January, leaving me two months to reorganize my budget.

Jump in and learn to swim, that's my motto.

Things worked out one more time. Board members and supporters came through with donations. Katie had already been helping us financially and gave us some extra money. Dr. Michelson contributed again. Erika Brunson threw a big fundraiser at her Bel-Air estate, bringing together activists and philanthropists to help us get a strong start in this new phase. Animal lovers who had been following SCIL's work stepped up.

With the details of his new role ironed out, Nick moved to Sacramento and started as SCIL's full-time Director of Legislative Affairs in January 2018.

The rest, as they say, is history.

Judie and Nick having a little fun in the Capitol.

Nick has been my eyes and ears on the ground ever since, taking in the big picture and all the details at the same time. It's Nick who takes our ideas and goals and translates them into good bills that become law. While just one person, Nick multiplied SCIL's capacity exponentially. Those eight bills we sponsored in 2018? They wouldn't have happened without Nick on the ground.

Wherever we went that first year with Nick on board, people would say, "Keep up the great work, everyone's talking about you!"

We certainly gave them a lot to talk about.

Welcome to the thunderdome of politics, Nick.

■ ■ ■

Of the eight bills SCIL sponsored in 2018, one died in committee, one was tabled, three were vetoed, and three became law.

People don't realize what an extraordinary success rate that is—or how much work it represents. We have to promote good laws and fight bad ones at the same time, all while moving forward on resolutions, budget items, and other issues.

One of our many under-the-radar accomplishments in 2018 was securing $7.5 million in the California state budget to address the problem of whale and sea turtle entanglements. SCIL board member Leah Sturgis, working with one of our main contract lobbyists, led that effort, marking a huge win for ocean wildlife.

Under the Trump administration, it felt like protections for animals were being repealed every day. SCIL organized a press conference to raise awareness. It got great attention thanks to the celebrities who participated. From left to right: Michelle Rodriguez, Katie Cleary, LA City Councilmember Paul Koretz, Joaquin Phoenix, State Senator Kevin de León, me, Simone Reyes, and Patty Shenker.

It wasn't all success that year, though. It still pains me to think about Governor Jerry Brown taking his veto pen to Senate Bill 1487, the Iconic African Species Protection Act. We had brought such a big coalition together to convince legislators there was no need for anyone in California to possess any body parts or skins of African species that were endangered, threatened, or vulnerable. I'm talking about elephants, lions, leopards, rhinoceroses, giraffes, zebras—animals that kids grow up dreaming about and that people claim to love but, when it comes down to it, refuse to protect. We came *so* close to getting California to stand up for those species. Working with our friends at the Center for Biological Diversity (CBD), we came up with language for a law that would be workable and enforceable. Appropriate exceptions would be granted for universities and a few other institutions.

On the other hand, hunters would no longer be allowed to bring their trophies into California.

The year before, in 2017, the US Department of Fish and Wildlife had announced its reversal of an Obama-era ban on importing elephant trophies from Zimbabwe and Zambia. Public uproar was immediate. SCIL organized a press conference outside LA City Hall, calling on the administration to reverse course. In addition to elected officials, including then-State Senate President pro tempore Kevin de León and LA City Councilmember Paul Koretz, actors Michelle Rodriguez and Joaquin Phoenix came to show support, which helped us get press coverage. CBD's Candice Kim announced that her organization had already filed a federal lawsuit to stop the reversal.

All this outcry earned us a short reprieve, but three months later, the ban was quietly repealed anyways. Trump's cabinet and family were full of men with deep ties to trophy hunting. They had won the day.

Our Iconic African Species Act almost became law in 2018. But at the last minute, the California Department of Fish and Wildlife was able to convince the governor that it would be too complex and expensive to enforce. Just like that—vetoed.

How soul-crushing it was to put so much work into a righteous cause that would have made such a big difference, only to have it erased with the stroke of a pen. We all teared up when we heard the news. Knowing you're bound to lose some battles doesn't make it hurt less when it happens.

Fortunately, we had some major victories to help heal the wound. Three of our sponsored bills were signed into law. A new record for SCIL! One was fairly technical, but the other two were game-changing for people, pets, and the planet.

■ ■ ■

California has long had a law on the books called the Pet Breeder Warranty Act, also known as the Puppy Lemon Law. It affords certain protections to consumers if they purchase animals with serious health or behavioral problems from breeders. Our puppy mill bill had made much of the language in it obsolete. So we sponsored Assembly Bill 2445, authored once again by Assemblymember Patrick O'Donnell, to ensure that consumers would enjoy the same protections if they adopted shelter animals from pet stores.

It was mostly a technical matter, a "clean-up bill," as it's known, but we had to go through the same process as for other bills, minus the intensive lobbying since there was no opposition.

AB 2445 was signed by the governor in July 2018, giving us our first success of the year.

The ideas for the other two SCIL bills that got signed into law that year came from a conversation I had with Dr. Neal Barnard at a gala for Dr. Gary Michelson's Found Animals Foundation. For decades, I had admired Dr. Barnard and his work with the Physicians Committee for Responsible Medicine (PCRM), which he founded in 1985. A truly powerful force in the animal rights world, PCRM has a vast alliance of 17,000 physicians and hundreds of thousands of volunteers that organize actions across the globe to stop animal cruelty, mostly by promoting plant-based eating and nonanimal testing methods.

There aren't many animal rights groups that are exactly what they say they are and do everything they do for the right reasons. PETA and CBD are examples. So is PCRM.

Besides being amazing philanthropists, wonderful people, generous souls, and staunch defenders of animal rights, Dr. Gary Michelson and Dr. Neal Barnard had in common that they had both refused to do research on animals in medical school, at the risk of getting kicked out.

Now that's what I call being an ally to animals.

Imagine my delight when Dr. Barnard came up to me at the gala and started the conversation by congratulating *me* on everything SCIL was doing! This kind of recognition is so energizing. I had the same feeling when I first started speaking to PETA President Ingrid Newkirk as a partner who admired and supported our work.

When Dr. Barnard floated the idea of PCRM and SCIL working together on legislation to end animal testing, he didn't have to ask twice. This had always seemed like one of the most egregious forms of animal abuse to me. I had long dreamed of putting an end to it, but how could little old me take on such a monumental issue?

After talking to Dr. Barnard, suddenly it felt like there might be *a lot* little old me could do.

I followed up first thing Monday. Dr. Barnard's staff was as anxious to get started as we were.

■ ■ ■

During our first meeting, each of us laid out what we'd like to get done in an ideal world and what we thought we could realistically accomplish. Plant-based nutrition is a top priority for PCRM, as it is for us. Could we mandate plant-based meals as an option in public schools, prisons, and hospitals?

We ran the idea by State Senator Nancy Skinner, who had offered to carry a bill for us. Schools were a nonstarter, she said. Just getting them to serve fresh fruit had been a Herculean battle. Mandating a vegan option wouldn't fly.

So we kept brainstorming to narrow the bill down to what was feasible. If we went with just medical and carceral facilities, the bill might get through. Easy to support, hard to oppose. More people than ever were reducing their meat and dairy consumption or going all the way vegan, and the movement was gathering steam. Requiring

SB 1138 kickoff press conference with Genesis Butler, Senator Nancy Skinner, and me.

that at least one plant-based option be offered to those who were confined in state healthcare facilities or prisons was reasonable. That's what we'd ask for.

When you're crafting groundbreaking laws, as SCIL likes to do, defining the scope of each bill is all-important. Of course, I'm a big believer in not taking no for an answer and going big when possible. But if the only alternative to incremental change is no change, I'll take a bit of progress every time. You have to be bold, but also pragmatic. Listen to what people with experience are telling you is doable. When someone as powerful as Senator Skinner says schools are off the table, take them off the table. We knew we could address that later through other means—and we did! The bill we introduced in 2022 to add a plant-based meal option in schools ended up becoming a budget item. For the 2023–24 school year, we led the effort to allow California schools to apply to get grants to cover the cost of adding meat- and dairy-free meals to their menus.

Senate Bill 1138, Ensuring a Plant-based Meal Option, authored by Senator Nancy Skinner and cosponsored by SCIL and PCRM, was introduced in February 2018.

We were expecting the entire meat and dairy industry to attack the bill. That would be par for the course. Whatever we do, they label us as extremists and rally the troops against us. So when the representative from the Cattlemen's Association showed up at the first committee hearing to say his group wouldn't oppose the bill, I nearly fell out of my chair. What on earth was going on? They *always* fought us on *everything*.

Turns out the one issue they really cared about was the preamble. That's where the author explains why a bill is necessary. The language isn't included in the final text, so it's never written into code. It might be considered if a judge is trying to interpret legislative intent, but it's not part of the law.

In the original preamble, the author mentioned the carcinogenic effects of meat and dairy products. Everything written was true and well-documented, and as good a reason as any to offer a plant-based option in state hospitals and prisons. But it didn't go over well with the factory farm crowd. Overnight, the committee started getting letters with the names of different cattle and poultry farm interests across the top—we call them "NASCAR letters" because they've got so many logos on them—complaining about the preamble. The hospital lobby ended up getting in on the action too.

Once we took out references to the health threats posed by meat and dairy, the bill made it through with no opposition. Governor Brown signed it into law on September 18, 2018.

This was such a sweet victory for us and PCRM. Here we were encouraging people to stop eating animal products, but in some settings, they had no other options. SB 1138 gave those who wanted to follow a plant-based diet, whether for health reasons or because they care about saving animals and the planet, the ability to do so. A similar law has since been passed in New York.

It's exactly how SCIL likes to operate: set the precedent and watch others follow.

CHAPTER 11

TIME TO GO BIG OR GO HOME, PART TWO

Every ounce of firepower our opponents held back on the plant-based meals bill got unleashed during our second effort with PCRM in 2018, Senate Bill 1249, the California Cruelty-Free Cosmetics Act, which would come to be known as the "cosmetics bill."

With this campaign, we set out to shake up the $500 billion-a-year global cosmetic industry by making California the first state in the nation to ban the sale of animal-tested cosmetic and personal hygiene products or ingredients.

Animal testing has been widely used in the United States since the late 1930s, when the Food and Drug Administration (FDA) introduced new safety substantiation requirements that led cosmetic companies to start testing their products on animals.

Early tests were unbelievably cruel and totally unscientific. Labs systematically tortured and killed hundreds of thousands of animals for results that couldn't consistently predict toxic responses in humans due to biological differences. Eighty years later, their methods were every bit as inhumane. To this day, rabbits, mice, guinea pigs, and other sentient beings are kept in tiny cages and subjected to painful tests for their whole, short lives. They are force-fed products to see if they develop organ damage or die (many do). Liquids are dripped into their eyes to see if irritation ensues. If the animals end up going blind (not uncommon), they're killed and replaced. Their fur is shaved off, and products are rubbed directly onto their skin to test for sensitivity. Once the lab is done with them, the animals are dumped in the trash, and often left to suffocate and writhe in pain because euthanizing them is too time-consuming and adds nothing to the bottom line.

For these animals, life is all about experiencing soreness, pain, terror, and misery in tiny cages before being tossed aside like inanimate objects. All so cosmetic companies can get consumers to buy "new and improved" products.

When SB 1249 was introduced, nonanimal tests were widely available. PCRM was doing more than anyone to ensure that scientists, governments, and industry around the world were aware of and migrating to these alternatives.

Animal rights advocates had been working in earnest since the 1970s to raise public awareness about the torture inflicted on animals in labs and how to stop it. PETA maintained a searchable database of cosmetic companies that do and don't test their ingredients and products on animals. Its "Beauty Without Bunnies" program gives consumers the ability to put their money where their values are and help end the suffering. More companies are added to its *Does Not Test* list every year.

Crucially, the nonanimal tests PCRM and others promote are cheaper, faster, and more reliable than animal-based ones.

Otherwise, the legislation couldn't pass. Computer models are actually more accurate predictors of human reactions. Three-dimensional human skin tissues and other types of cells engineered by scientists for testing purposes work better than animal tissues and cells.

The PCRM toxicologists who helped us shepherd the bill through the legislature spent hours explaining all this to me, to Nick, to our lobbyists, and to lawmakers. Having them with us in the initial meetings with the opposition and in committee hearings changed everything. Cosmetic companies could whine all day about their options being limited. PCRM experts were there to make sure the lawmakers who'd be voting on the bill knew there was a whole alternative testing ecosystem just waiting to be explored.

In sum, businesses had every opportunity to grow and thrive without animal testing. They just needed a push in the right direction. The cosmetics bill would give them that push.

■ ■ ■

A fairly concrete idea of what we could ask for had emerged from our first brainstorming sessions with PCRM. Proceeding by process of elimination, we looked at everything that had been done in California, in other states, and in other countries.

California has a long history of leadership in promoting alternatives to animal tests. In 2000, it became the first state to outlaw the use of animals for tests when appropriate alternatives were available, though it was still legal to import and sell cosmetics tested on animals. That's what we were going after now.

In 2014, the legislature adopted the Cruelty-Free Cosmetics Resolution, urging Congress to ban animal tests for cosmetics and to phase out the marketing of animal-tested products. Years of inaction at the federal level followed. In the meantime, almost forty countries had begun requiring nonanimal tests. The European Union banned animal tests for cosmetics and personal care products in 2009 and in 2013 forbade the sale or marketing of cosmetic products and ingredients tested on animals.

Progress was being made elsewhere toward phasing out these barbaric tests, yet no such restrictions applied in the United States. Companies that continued to rely on cruel, antiquated, and ineffective animal testing methods were still able to market their ingredients and finished products across the country, including in California.

Polling made it abundantly clear that public opinion was on our side. Much of the scientific community, and a growing number of businesses, concurred that animal testing was unethical and archaic and had no place in our modern society. Consumers were actively seeking out products that boasted the cruelty-free label, guaranteeing that their production involved no animal testing at any stage.

Despite the ready availability of nonanimal testing methods and having access to tens of thousands of ingredients already approved as safe, some manufacturers continued to support the torture and killing of animals through their supply chains.

Now, riding the success of the puppy mill bill and building on all the work that had been done by others before us, we were ready to take California's $3.5 billion-a-year cosmetic market out of the equation for those companies.

■ ■ ■

Shortly after we decided to move forward with the cosmetics bill, the lobbyist who had been by my side since 2007 informed me she had a conflict of interest since she also represented one of the cosmetic companies opposing the bill. It caught me completely off guard. I'd gotten so used to having her in my corner, and trusting her, I'd just assumed we'd be going into this fight together.

She suggested that the best person to replace her was David Quintana, a man with a big reputation in Sacramento and a pillar of California's Third House. *Capitol Weekly's* Top 100 for 2015 described David as a character who, of all the lobbyists in Sacramento, was "perhaps the most like something dreamed up by a TV screenwriter." I would agree. Having served in the military for ten years and held a series of jobs across multiple industries before going back to school and getting his law degree, David was extraordinarily comfortable in conflict situations. Nothing fazed him, it seemed. He was mostly known for representing tribal gaming and cannabis interests. And for throwing epic parties. It was David who created the annual "Back to Session Bash," a mega event where legislators, staffers, and lobbyists hobnob, drink free booze, and enjoy world-class entertainment, usually big-name rappers and hip-hop artists. It's a who's who of California lobbyists and powerbrokers, and it's known as *the* place to be and be seen in January.

Our first meeting was a scene straight out of a movie. Or a documentary about political power and influence. The lobbyist introducing me to David had booked a patio table for three at the swanky Montage Resort up the road from my home in Laguna Beach. David arrived after we did, and as I watched him move toward us across the patio, bald head, stocky frame, custom suit complete with pocket square, eyes hidden behind aviator sunglasses, I thought, *I can see where he gets his reputation.*

Brief pleasantries exchanged, we got down to business. David had dogs and cats, and usually a couple of fosters rotating through his house. I quickly saw that he had the compassion gene that animal lovers share. He knew what our bill would do and what a big deal it would be, and he was ready to take on what was sure to be a major, messy fight.

I hired him that day.

Paul Bauer, another powerful lobbyist whose reputation preceded him, came on board next, at David's suggestion. One of David's assistants, Caity Maple, now a Sacramento City Councilmember, was assigned to the bill full time. She had been in the business for a few years, so she'd be able to help teach Nick the ropes, show him some basics like doing floor alerts, counting votes, and "walking the halls" (basically, going door to door in the Capitol to promote your bill and pitching everyone you run into along the way). The other seasoned pros we were working with on other bills also helped Nick ease into his new role, as did I. I still enjoy sharing my years of experience with him.

I am still learning too. Every lobbyist I've ever hired has taught me some aspect of advocacy that makes me more effective. How to watch body language and read between the lines when interacting with lawmakers. How sometimes, if you're paying attention, you can see that they're saying no, but also laying out breadcrumbs to show you how to take a different route to where you want to go.

Once, I made the mistake of talking strategy to a lobbyist in a crowded elevator. As soon as we were alone, she explained that in Sacramento, I needed to assume that every time I spoke, every person within earshot was working to defeat my bills and would use everything they heard against me.

Besides being a fierce lobbyist, David taught me the importance of relationships in getting laws passed. We'll never be as big or have as much money as some of the national animal rights groups. That is a reality. And we'll often find ourselves up against companies and special interest groups with deep pockets. But here in California, working on the ground, we can create the relationships that level the playing field, or at least make it a little more even.

It's what we would do for the cosmetics bill and it's how we would win. They had more money, but we would have more friends.

We started pitching the idea for a cosmetics bill to lawmakers' offices in January. My good friend from Senator Dean Florez's office, Bob Alvarez, was Senator Cathleen Galgiani's chief of staff at the time, and he was fairly certain she'd be interested, given her compassion for and interest in animals. She immediately agreed to carry the bill.

On February 15, 2018, the California Cruelty-Free Cosmetics Act, authored by Senator Cathleen Galgiani and cosponsored by SCIL and PCRM, was introduced.

■ ■ ■

Word quickly got around that a big animal bill was in the works. Like clockwork, Senator Galgiani called within a few weeks to ask about all the people coming out of the woodwork to scream about her bill. Special interests, I told her. And they're just getting started. Their numbers will grow, and they will escalate—you can count on it. She asked Bob to organize a meeting with all the stakeholders so everyone could get the lay of the land. Great news for us. We needed to see who we were up against and what angles they planned to attack us from.

As a fairly high-ranking senator, Senator Galgiani had a spacious office—round table with four chairs, couch and coffee table. We'd been in it many times and it always looked so big. Not that day. Every inch of wall space was filled by lobbyists for the other side. Extra chairs had been brought in to accommodate them, but some still had to stand—a packed house for our bill! Many had flown in from other states just for that meeting.

Putting on a show of force is effective sometimes, and they certainly pulled it off that day. It wasn't by chance that our opponents took the spots around the edges of the room and left us the ones in the middle. We were literally surrounded.

Most Sacramento meetings start with an endless exchange of business cards. It took several minutes to make the rounds that day.

The cards handed to us told quite a story. Huge multinationals with combined market capitalization of well over a trillion dollars. It was the last time we'd see the names of those companies written down. As the bill moved forward, they would face off with us through proxies with names like Personal Care Products Council, American Chemistry Council, California Life Sciences Association. Front groups that opposed the bill out in the open while their members and clients hid in the shadows, pouring their endless resources into defeating us.

Me, Senator Cathleen Galgiani, Katie Cleary, and Kristie Sullivan after one of our first meetings hashing out the details of SB 1249.

The attitude from the lobbyists in that room was one I've experienced more times than I can say. Exasperation that such important people with such pressing business to attend to had to sit down with silly animal rights activists like us. How naïve we were to think we could get these giant corporations to stop

Top row, lobbyists Kristin Olsen and Paul Bauer. Bottom row, me, Elizabeth Baker, and Nick Sackett.

selling products tested on animals. We were way out of our league and wasting their time.

Paul and I sat on the couch with Kristie Sullivan, a toxicologist and PCRM's vice president of research policy. David and Nick sat at the table, poised to take notes on where the sticking points were likely to be.

Every person who worked on this bill was amazing and had a role in our success, but I don't see how we could have gotten it done without Kristie. She knew more about the issue than anyone in the room and could refute the other side's claims one by one. The whole PCRM crew also understood the regulatory landscape inside and out, which was invaluable. We were heading into uncharted waters with this bill, and they were our compass when it came to policy and science. Before going into that meeting, Nick and I spent hours on the phone with Kristie and Elizabeth Baker, PCRM's director of research policy, discussing every potential challenge, making every necessary tweak.

Another person who was absolutely central to our success was Kathy Guillermo, PETA's senior vice president, Laboratory Investigations Department, and a walking encyclopedia of all things animal testing. When I had spoken to PETA President Ingrid Newkirk about the bill very early on in the year, she promised to help in every way possible. The first thing she did was bring in Kathy, who would make herself available to us and work around the clock to help move the bill forward, with PETA's full weight behind her. There's no way to overstate how vital support from PETA was to this undertaking. It has millions of people on its mailing list and can segment recipients by district and zip code. That kind of targeted messaging was critical to our success.

Between PETA tapping into its list of supporters, and PCRM mobilizing the thousands of doctors and medical professionals who are committed to saving and protecting animals, our effort took on a whole new dimension.

Of course the cosmetic companies in that room had no idea what kind of support we'd be bringing. They expected to be able to shut us down right away. California represented billions of dollars of annual revenue for them, and the market was steadily growing. They wanted to continue to do business as usual in the Golden State, no matter how many animals died.

But now, through PCRM and SCIL, backed by PETA, Dr. Michelson, and animal groups and individuals throughout the state, the animals had a voice in the conversation.

■ ■ ■

During that first meeting in Senator Galgiani's office, Kristie and I set the stage with a brief pitch on what the bill would do and why it was necessary. With so many equivalent or superior nonanimal methods on the market, there was no reason for anyone to be torturing animals.

Modern versus antiquated. Reliable versus unreliable. Humane, sustainable practices versus ones that Californians massively disapprove of and see as barbaric. Following the lead of the European Union versus staying stuck in the previous century. That was how we presented the case.

Then we listened.

Initial meetings like this are fact-finding missions for us. The sooner we identify the potential obstacles, the more effectively we can address them. Most of the time we just have to sit there while our opponents use scare tactics about how the sky will fall if our bill passes. We've heard it all. Manufacturing plants will be shut down! Jobs will be shipped overseas! The world as we know it will end! Same song and dance every time. Sometimes it works. Lawmakers will do anything to avoid being seen as hurting business interests, even if the claims aren't true. Giving them the information they need to refute the other side's arguments is a huge part of our work. We need the legislators who vote on the bills we sponsor to support us confidently, armed with facts.

One thing we stipulated from the outset was that all ingredients and finished products already on the market would be grandfathered in. Legislators would never be able to live it down if they were accused of forcing companies to remove vast quantities of products from their inventories and store shelves. Our opponents would have had a field day railing against the cost of such efforts and the disruption to their supply chains and markets. The bill would have been DOA.

Besides, the damage was already done. Those ingredients had already been tested at the expense of animal lives. SB 1249 would only prohibit the sale of cosmetics *newly* tested on animals after January 1, 2020. The only thing these companies had to stop doing was needlessly torture animals when they developed new ingredients. Better for business, better for consumers, better for the animals. Everybody comes out ahead.

After discussing it at length with the PCRM team, we decided it would be counterproductive to include any other exceptions in the first iteration of the bill. Experience shows that exceptions quickly become loopholes, those loopholes become business models, and nothing changes.

As soon as the other side took the floor in Senator Galgiani's office, we saw their strategy: raise fears about jobs and supply chains. In the most condescending terms possible, they explained that their supply chains were way too complex for us to ever wrap our little heads around. Did we think they could monitor and control what every one of their suppliers did? What would we ask for next, that they send inspectors to every plant they purchased from? Why, at this rate, before you knew it, us crazy animal rights people would put them out of business.

Remember that each of these companies was worth hundreds of billions of dollars. And here they were suggesting that making this one change would eliminate tens of thousands of jobs and cause their entire supply chains to collapse.

Kristie had a counterargument for every talking point. The testing ecosystem is much narrower than what they were portraying. It's not like there are so many tiny firms doing animal testing that no one can keep track of them all. The multinationals in that room wouldn't do business with small labs anyway. They contracted with large firms that could easily have been pressured to switch to newer, humane, more effective testing methods.

But that day, we mostly listened, and took in the talking points the other side was going to be using against us.

■ ■ ■

Our other certainty after the first meeting was that China's animal testing regulations would be a major obstacle. It was a confusing issue for lawmakers, and our opponents would take full advantage of its complexity. I'll give a brief overview: China had changed its laws in 2014. Until then, all cosmetics produced or sold in the country had to be tested on animals. Starting in 2014, ordinary cosmetics like shampoos, nail polish, and makeup were exempted from pre-market testing rules. However—and this was the crux of the matter where our bill was concerned—the new rule only applied to domestic production. Imported products still had to be tested on animals, either in the producing country or in China. That was the official rule.

There were workarounds, as we would later show.

When SB 1249 was introduced, of the four tests officially required to sell in China, two were nonanimal. The country was moving away from that unpopular practice. The whole world was.

Nonetheless, the way the issue was being presented, and as confusing as it was, we knew it would be tough to stop lawmakers from carving out a huge exemption for China. The Chinese cosmetic market was worth close to $50 billion in 2018. If our bill was seen as blocking access to it, we would lose.

David, my star lobbyist, had gone up against his share of deep-pocketed corporations and knew how much numbers mattered in situations like this. After listening to our opponents make their case in that first meeting, he pulled me aside in the hallway.

"Judie, do you really want to get this bill done?"

"Yes. Absolutely."

"Well then, you're going to need to lobby up."

"Lobby up? What does that mean? I've got you and Paul and your teams and Nick."

"You saw how many people they have? It's like we're putting our little nuclear family up against a huge, organized army. We need to have as many soldiers as them. As many boots on the ground. That's going to be the name of the game in this fight. Big presence in every meeting, in every hearing, in every lawmaker's office, in every hallway."

Numbers were swirling in my head. This was not in my budget.

"How many are we talking about?"

"I'll let you know."

David went off and conferenced with his team. He came back and said, "Three to start."

Not counting the staff they brought with them. Definitely not in the budget.

I did the math and thought about how we'd have to ramp up even further ahead of the committee hearings. SCIL was potentially looking at an additional cost of $50,000 a month. I had just scaled up by hiring Nick, and now I had to lobby up too!

Panic overtook me. We had a solid bill that we knew could save millions of animals. The effect would be exponential. And here we were, at risk of getting kicked aside by special interests, just because our side couldn't raise as much money.

This is one of the most difficult realities I've had to accept: how exorbitantly expensive it is to get good laws passed and fight bad ones. It costs a fortune to be effective in the legislative arena, and that's by design. Why do so many people give up? Why do the little voices end up getting drowned out so often? Because smaller groups can't compete. They don't have that kind of money lying around. We certainly don't. Bigger animal protection groups have it, but they rarely spend it on legislation. Too much of a gamble for them. Way too much work. Instead, their funds go to things like executive pay and marketing campaigns.

My risk-reward calculation is totally different. I would rather be David taking on Goliath over and over than sitting in a cushy office, talking about all my grand plans. Every single animal saved by a SCIL-sponsored law strengthens my commitment to the mission. It's one of the main reasons I created SCIL in the first place—to fill that void in the legislative space.

I spent what felt like several days on the phone, dialing for dollars. PCRM came through with a massive donation. Dr. Michelson matched

Our stellar team of lobbyists helped us get SB 1249 over the finish line. We're smiling in these photos, but it was a nail-biter right up until the end!

it. Every time we asked PETA to help cover our mounting expenses, they stepped up. Small donors chipped in everything they could.

Within a week, we were ready to start putting that bigger army together. Soon we had six lobbyists, then eight, then ten.

Whenever lawmakers or their staff turned around, someone from Team SB 1249 was there, reminding them what the bill was about and that there was only one way to vote.

Some new and incredibly powerful allies were about to join us too.

■ ■ ■

Senator Galgiani's office was receiving mountains of support letters that her office passed on to us, since we were sponsors of the bill. (If you're one of the people who writes to lawmakers to encourage them to do the right thing, know that your letters make a world of difference.)

Two letters arrived in March that changed the whole trajectory of the bill for us. One was from global haircare brand John Paul Mitchell Systems (JPMS), expressing its support. JPMS had signed PETA's statement of assurance nearly thirty years earlier. It was known for its very public stance against animal testing. I reached out to founder John Paul DeJoria, and he asked how he could help.

Could he write testimony for me to read at a hearing on his behalf? Absolutely! He sent a letter laying out in detail how he had built a global haircare empire without hurting a single animal.

Ethical business was coming through one more time to help us build our case.

Multinational cosmetic firms were trying to scare the daylights out of lawmakers with stories about how they'd have to shut down all their North American factories and fire all their workers if our bill

Lush was all the way behind SB 1249 from day one. In 2019, they put me on the label of their Charity Pot floral scented body lotion, with my dogs Candy and Dinky, to help raise funds for grassroots groups like ours that support animal protection.

passed. In response, we would tell the story of a global brand that was thriving using only nonanimal tests. In fact, the cruelty-free stamp on JPMS haircare was the decisive factor in many people's decision to purchase its products. Consumers overwhelmingly oppose animal testing, and the companies that pledge to not participate in it can get ahead by delivering good products people feel good about using. JPMS was proof.

It's the only haircare brand I've used for more than forty years.

The second letter that caught my eye was from Lush Cosmetics. I knew about the company's position on animal rights and loved its products, but we hadn't reached out to ask them to support the bill. Luckily for us, as a brand that lives its values, Lush has people on staff who track initiatives that are aligned with its cause to see how it can help.

Hence its unsolicited letter in support of SB 1249, signed by Hilary Pickles, the company's charitable giving ambassador.

I called her right away and introduced myself.

"We love your bill," Hilary said. "Tell us what we can do." Music to my ears! Could she help us grow our coalition? Hilary sent an email to everyone who had donated to Lush's charitable fund and asked for letters of support, which we got. Would she also be willing to speak directly to lawmakers about how Lush manages its supply chain? Hilary flew in for the first committee hearing and delivered some of the most compelling testimony we could get about humane business models and corporate responsibility.

When business gets involved, the whole conversation changes. We'd seen it with the puppy mill bill. Once Andrew Kim testified about how his pet store chain had boomed from day one without ever doing business with breeders, lawmakers began to listen in a different way. It's their job to seek the best possible outcome for all stakeholders. If they have an opportunity to create the space for businesses to grow while also saving animals, then that's exactly how they're supposed to vote.

I can't describe how motivating it was to address lawmakers for the first time with such powerful allies by my side. Animal rights campaigns can be brutal and are oftentimes lonely. How many times had I left a meeting after fighting to get even one word in? How many times had I been treated like a nuisance people wanted to get rid of so they could get back to business as usual?

Going into the committee hearings for SB 1249, we had PCRM bringing world-class medical expertise to the table, PETA working for us behind the scenes with its expertise and support base, and JPMS and Lush explaining cruelty-free models from a business standpoint.

Without these partners, SCIL would have been just another group of activists trying to stop animal testing. With them, we were a leading force in the animal rights space.

CHAPTER 12

SETTING GLOBAL STANDARDS

As written when it was introduced on February 15, 2018, the California Cruelty-Free Cosmetics Act included the grandfather clause, but no other exceptions. That meant that the day the new law went into effect, any products newly tested on animals would be banned from sale in California, even if only one ingredient was newly tested, and even if the testing occurred outside a manufacturer's supply chain.

Based on what we'd taken away from that March meeting with opponents and the exchanges we'd had with them since, we made several author's amendments early in April, three weeks before the bill went to its first committee hearing. It's a bit complicated, but the details are important, so bear with me.

First, we would allow companies to get an exemption from the ban if the FDA or California Department of Toxic Substances required animal testing. (The FDA does not officially require animal tests for cosmetics, but we thought it best to avoid that argument preemptively.)

Second, animal testing would be allowed if there was no alternative method available *and* no substitute ingredient available. That latter point was crucial. Remember, tens of thousands of ingredients were being grandfathered in, many of them already tested on animals. Manufacturers were spoiled for choice. We didn't want to give them the opportunity to say they needed to develop product X, for which no alternative testing was available, when product Y, an exact equivalent, was available. The amendment cut off that possibility.

Our third concession was a big one: products tested on animals to comply with a formal request from a foreign regulatory authority (yes, such as China) could continue to be sold in California, but the exemption would sunset on January 1, 2023. Manufacturers thus had five years to adopt new testing methods and work with Chinese authorities to find a way to get their products into that market without testing on animals. Most experts assumed the testing requirements would change before the exemption expired in 2023 anyway, since China was already moving in that direction, but we wanted to allay fears about that.

Remember, the cosmetic companies opposing the bill were saying they wanted to end animal testing, claiming they would if they could. Well, we were giving them the chance to put their money where their mouth was. A five-year window to use some of the tens of billions of dollars they had in the bank to get suppliers to adopt newer, cheaper, and more reliable testing methods and transition to a cruelty-free model.

Sounds reasonable, doesn't it? Were they serious about ending animal testing or not?

■ ■ ■

Senate Judiciary was the first committee to hold a hearing on the bill. Senator Galgiani kicked things off by reminding members that, just four years earlier, many of them had supported Senate Joint Resolution 22, which urged Congress to pass the Humane Cosmetics Act to prohibit the sale of animal-tested cosmetic products nationwide. Historically, when Congress failed to act, California took the lead. That's what Senator Galgiani was asking her colleagues to do now.

After the author presents their bill at a committee hearing, each side can have two primary witnesses speak for two minutes each. A microphone is set up for add-on witnesses (commonly known as "me toos") to voice their support or opposition for the record.

After Senator Galgiani, Hilary Pickles from Lush Cosmetics made the case that manufacturers could build thriving businesses without ever harming a single animal. Lush had been in business for more than twenty years and had over two hundred shops in North America, including forty in California. Its growth over two decades had been impressive. She drew a straight line between that success and the values the company upheld. More than 600 North American cosmetic brands certified as cruelty-free were doing well. Lush had written its nonanimal testing policy to exclude any suppliers that tested on animals anywhere in the world, for any purpose, including non-cosmetic ones.

It lived its values by keeping a close eye on every part of its supply chain.

Up next was Kristie Sullivan, PCRM's vice president of research policy, who led with a graphic description of the Draize animal test. Developed in 1944 and still in use today, this test involves dropping or spraying chemicals into the eyes of restrained rabbits and observing them for twenty-four hours to see how much pain, swelling, or discharge they experience—or if they go blind. The test is done on rabbits because they do not produce tears, meaning there's no physiological mechanism for their bodies to naturally wash the products from their eyes. Unlike humans, their bodies can't protect them from the discomfort and pain. I watched lawmakers react as Kristie described the test. She had their attention. Her pivot to the solution was seamless. "Fortunately, nonanimal test methods based on human corneal skin, immune cells, and other human cells and tissues are widely available to use in place of this and other tests. In fact, nonanimal methods for skin allergy perform better and are more accurate than the original animal tests."

The case was laid out. Animal tests were cruel. Manufacturers had access to other tests that were not cruel and better adapted for cosmetic products. So why were companies still using them? According to Kristie, it was because of institutional resistance and regulatory expediency. Not good reasons.

"Citizens understand that animals shouldn't suffer for the newest wrinkle cream or shampoo scent," she concluded. "This bill creates that beautiful future."

Five people came to the microphone to express their support. Katie Cleary, who was a SCIL board member at the time, stated her name and simply said, "We want cruelty-free products. These animals are tortured."

The mood was set.

The first witness in opposition to the bill was the lobbyist for the Personal Care Products Council (PCPC). Her testimony was as expected: cosmetic manufacturers were against animal testing in principle and had been leading the way in this field for decades.

According to her, the companies that used animal-tested ingredients in their products were the real heroes here, investing hundreds of millions of dollars to reduce or eliminate animal testing (all while carrying on with business as usual). But they couldn't support this bill because it went too far. We heard the exact same nonsense every time. *You're asking for too much too soon! Let us keep doing what we're doing and we'll get there in our own time! We give you an inch, you take a mile! At this rate, you'll put us all out of business!*

Predictably, the top complaint of the cosmetic companies' proxies was the China exception. The PCPC lobbyist painted a bleak picture: once the exemption expired, manufacturers would have to choose between selling in China or selling in California. Of course she warned that this would impact small manufacturers, but we all knew she was being paid to represent some of the biggest companies in the world. Companies that could go cruelty-free without missing a beat.

A lobbyist for the Household and Commercial Products Association and International Fragrance Association of North America spoke next. She brought up another big sticking point: under our bill, products could not be sold in California if any ingredient in them had been tested anywhere in the world for any purpose, including non-cosmetic ones. She mentioned pesticides. Yes, there is overlap between pesticide and cosmetic manufacturing—not an appealing thought, I know. Home care products too. Disinfectants are classified as pesticides, which need to be tested on animals. So for instance, ingredients tested on rodents in university research for pesticides would be barred from use in cosmetics.

Alternatives to the ingredients she was talking about existed for cosmetics, but of course she didn't mention that.

Both lobbyists for the other side said they supported the EU model, which allows products into the market even if certain ingredients have been tested on animals, as long as the testing is done to comply with the request of another government—you guessed it, China.

Their add-on witnesses were a who's who of manufacturers and retailers: California Chamber of Commerce, American Chemistry Council, Chemical Industry Council, and others. People who were, in this instance, getting paid to defend the status quo while claiming that their clients were working to change it.

I can tell you that the concerns expressed about the China exception were not lost on committee members. One senator immediately ran with the fantasy scenario presented by the opposition in which a company opens a plant in China to be able to sell there, but sees its products banned in California after 2023 when the exemption expires. Kristie pointed out just how unlikely this scenario was. A growing number of nonanimal tests were being developed and accepted by regulators. Chances were that it would be a moot point by 2023.

Committee Chair Senator Hannah-Beth Jackson backed us up beautifully by pointing out that when asked for proof of the kinds of testing China was requiring, such as copies of the regulations, the opposition submitted a five-hundred-page document . . . in Chinese. "I find it very hard to believe that with all the money this industry generates, with all the legal people power it has, they couldn't actually translate this for us," she said. "That's the kind of thing that really creates a serious credibility gap. So I'm going to take the position that this isn't even a problem since we have no proof that it is, other than in Chinese."

Bad move on the opposition's part. Note to those trying to get legislation passed in California or anywhere: don't try to underpin your argument with documentation lawmakers can't read.

We were thrilled with Senator Jackson's response, but the fight was far from over. A follow-up question about why our bill went further than the EU ban gave Kristie a chance to explain that the animal testing ecosystem is fairly small, and that most of the testing that takes place happens within the gaping hole left open by the EU law. Given the chance, manufacturers would keep waltzing right through that hole.

Again, Senator Jackson understood exactly what Kristie was saying and summed it up for her colleagues: "So the EU contract ruling allows the China exemption, and you're saying that creates a huge hole and effectively neutralizes the impacts of the effort."

Exactly.

The final vote was 5-to-1, with an abstention recorded from John Moorlach of Orange County. After the hearing, I reminded him that he could have voted yes, that he had nothing to be afraid of. "John's afraid of everything," someone quipped. Even John laughed. It was true. John *was* afraid of everything. He was known for abstaining even on noncontroversial bills. And he represented my district. I'd led a group of constituents to his district office to urge him to support the bill. He still sat it out.

Fear was something we had to deal with every day. I've seen lawmakers take a stand for animals and refuse to back down no matter what kind of opposition they face. Unfortunately, profiles in courage are very rare. It's so much more comfortable for them on the sidelines. And that's where too many of the assemblymembers and senators we deal with choose to stay.

■ ■ ■

Next stop: Senate Appropriations on May 14. It was a vital hurdle. Our opponents were working around the clock, behind the scenes, tapping into their bottomless coffers to pressure lawmakers to vote no. Wining and dining them. Making promises. David reminded me every day that we needed to grab people's attention. The opposition had unlimited dough. Because we'd never be able to keep pace on that front, we had to come up with better ideas.

At his suggestion, we took over the homepage of the *Sacramento Bee* during the twenty-four hours before the hearing. All nine ads on that page were ours. They showed the barbaric nature of animal testing, in graphic detail. A couple of the images our team pitched to us were too grisly for the public. But the ones we used got the point across. Bunnies pinned in place so they couldn't move a muscle no matter how bad the pain got. A woman applying lipstick with blood dripping down her chin. Whoever went on the website that day got confronted with these images. And everyone in the Capitol was on that website every day. Walking through the hallways, we'd see people wince as our ads popped up on their phones and computers. By design, the ads were right in their faces, reminding them of exactly what the bill was about.

The campaign was anchored by a video—also unavoidable when anyone looked at their screens—featuring Alicia Silverstone, Moby, Harley Quinn Smith, Genesis Butler, Jane Velez-Mitchell, Kristie Sullivan, Dr. Neal Barnard, and me, talking about how cruel and simply unnecessary animal testing is. Were they for or against this needless suffering? Their votes would be their answer.

An analysis of the bill put the financial impact above the threshold, triggering its transfer to the suspense file, which is like a legislative black hole. Once bills go onto that file, you never know if they're going to come off again. SCIL and Senator Galgiani successfully fought to rescue it, which was a victory in and of itself. SB 1249 could have died right then and there.

Appropriations considered it two weeks later with just one minor technical amendment on the FDA exemption. Otherwise, it was the same bill the Judiciary Committee had approved. It passed on a 5-to-2 vote. Both noes were from Republicans, whose party had taken an official stand against us. We had some resistance from Democrats as well. One Democratic senator from Orange County was facing a recall and needed money. A cosmetic company proxy held a fundraiser for him, and he flipped. Not officially, mind you. Rather, he suddenly started asking all kinds of questions and saying he needed more information and time to think and hey, what about that China exemption, would that maybe be a good idea? I knew he'd gone over to the dark side. Talk about disappointing. This was someone who had carried a bill for us and been an ally. We'd even given him an award the year before! A few other Democrats had reservations as well. One made plain that animals were not his priority, so we shouldn't even talk to him about any bills focused on them.

SB 1249 wasn't a partisan battle for us. We had to utilize every tool in the toolbox and move mountains to get support on both sides of the aisle.

■ ■ ■

Next came the monumental challenge of getting the bill through the Senate floor vote scheduled for May 30. We were up to twelve lobbyists on our team by then, all of whom had existing relationships with people in the Capitol. Based on their personal connections, I dispatched them to talk to lawmakers, answer questions, address concerns, work with staff, reiterate what our bill would and wouldn't do, work the votes, then work the votes some more.

Our opponents had all the money in the world and were handing out donations and promises, but we had good relationships with lawmakers. They trusted us and knew we talked straight. I brought on a former GOP assemblymember who had joined a public relations consulting firm. It's a sad reality that people can go back and forth between holding government jobs and working as lobbyists. The practice is totally legal, and it's nearly impossible to get things done if you take a principled stand not to hire from the revolving door while your opponents are doing it. The former assemblymember who joined our team was tasked with bringing Republicans over to yes. Some of our lobbyists had worked closely with senators on other issues in the past, and they were assigned to get those votes.

By the end of May, we were a well-oiled machine. As we do for every bill, we kept a scorecard. Who's a definite yes? Definite no? Leaning no but persuadable? Each senator's position was noted and tracked.

At the same time, our core team was exploring ways to pull in influential people who could help get us votes. One senator was a huge baseball fan. Katie Cleary had a friend who played in the majors. She got the player to send an email to the senator, asking him to vote for the bill. We had supporters attend lawmakers' ice cream socials and fundraisers and other events to remind them that they had an opportunity to be on the right side of history with SB 1249. Op-eds were published in papers up and down the state to raise awareness and get people to pay attention to where their representatives stood on the issue.

In addition to being more creative than the opposition, we had more celebrities on our side. I'd love to say it was our brilliant strategizing and tireless efforts alone that ultimately got the bill through the Senate, but that wouldn't be the whole story. We certainly put in the hours and laid the groundwork. In the end, however, pure star power got us over the finish line in the form of a very special guest who showed up the day of the Senate floor vote.

Going into that session, our opponents were certain they were going to kill the bill. Their scorecard showed that every Republican was locked in as a no. As far as they were concerned, it was over. They never saw Maggie Q coming.

I had known Maggie through animal rights work for almost ten years. She is as fierce a defender of animals as anyone and a real leader in this space. When Hurricane Harvey struck Texas in 2017, Katie Cleary went there with fellow SCIL board member Simone Reyes to help rescue animals. They stayed at the home of the baseball player who'd sent the email for us. Maggie was there as well, and they all connected around animal rights. She knew about SCIL and had supported our efforts in the past.

When she asked if there was anything she could do to help with SB 1249, we didn't hesitate: Are you busy on May 30?

There's a low wooden gate at the end of the hallway leading to the chamber. It's carefully guarded to keep lobbyists out when the Senate is in session. If you want to have a last-minute conversation with a senator before a vote, that's where you wait. It's all done by text message now, but when I first started out, you had to write your message on a card and have it delivered by the sergeant-at-arms. "Super important, two minutes max. Please!" Of course, they were free to ignore such messages, but sometimes they would come out and talk to you there in the hallway or in one of the private rooms nearby.

I've gotten votes at the last minute near that gate. I've talked members into flipping colleagues there too.

That day, we had two reasons for staying close to the gate. First, we needed to know who the opposition was working on. Which meant keeping an eye on the door to the chamber until the official session started. Nick was nearby, sitting on the floor, back against the wall, fingers hovering over the keyboard of his laptop with the text of the bill on the screen, ready to make last-minute amendments if we needed to.

The other reason we were there? We knew starstruck senators wouldn't be able to resist stopping by to see Maggie Q. And stop by they did! Including two Republicans whose votes were considered locked in for the other side. When they gushed about how much they loved Maggie's work, she thanked them and said she was there because of her love for animals.

You could feel the energy shift. My heart was smiling, but my face couldn't show it since our opponents had people posted by the gate to watch our every move. They had been following us around for months. It was like being in a spy movie. Every time we went into an office to talk to a lawmaker, they'd wait until we left, then slip in to find out what was said and if a vote had been swayed. Of course they couldn't hear the conversation with Maggie Q. Even if they suspected it might be about the bill, they couldn't be sure what to do about it.

Before you knew it, the two senators who'd come to talk to Maggie nodded to us and went into the chamber. Doing my best to keep a poker face, I texted David, who was waiting upstairs in the balcony, to let him know there was a possibility Maggie had broken through the solid wall the opposition had built around Republicans and gotten two more votes.

Climbing the stairs to watch the floor session from the gallery, we knew we still might be a few votes short, including the Orange County Democrat who'd flipped—the one I'd given that award to. We held our breath as we watched the senators move around on the red carpet below, joking with one another, laughing, whispering, reading on their tablets.

If we didn't get to twenty-one yes votes, it would all end there.

Just as the session was starting, a San Diego Democrat we'd had a hard time pinning down lifted his eyes toward us and gave the thumbs up. He pointed to a colleague who'd been resistant and indicated that he, too, was now a yes.

We could hardly believe our eyes. SB 1249 was successfully voted off the Senate floor, 21-to-9, with nine not voting.

■ ■ ■

While the Senate was clearly the biggest hurdle for us, we weren't out of the woods. As expected, our victory set off a flurry of activity on the other side. They were out for blood now. The bill's next stop was the Assembly Judiciary Committee hearing on June 26. It was a friendly committee, but we'd still need to work hard for every vote.

Hilary was the first witness for our side. She retold the story of how Lush became an incredibly successful company and attributed that success in large part to its 100 percent cruelty-free model. Since the medical aspects of the bill weren't being disputed anymore, and the focus was mostly on supply chains, we decided that I would be the second witness. PCRM's Elizabeth Baker was in the room in case we needed her for science questions.

The package we submitted to lawmakers before the hearing included a list of more than three thousand companies around the world that operated with no animal testing anywhere on their supply chains. They ranged in size from very small to very large. At the top of the list was JPMS, with its annual revenue of more than a billion dollars.

As I began my testimony by reading the letter John Paul DeJoria had written for us, you could hear a pin drop. I reminded the committee that in voting yes on SB 1249, they would be upholding the will of their constituents. Californians, especially the younger generations who represent the future of our state and country, overwhelmingly oppose all forms of institutionalized animal cruelty, including testing.

This time, we had a long line of add-on witnesses step up to the microphone. Several people from PCRM. One woman who'd come all the way from Washington, DC, just to state her support. Volunteers for rescues and spay and neuter groups. Katie Cleary, Jane-Velez Mitchell, and other celebrities. Teachers and students. People who had rescued lab animals. It was an incredible display of passion and compassion.

Watching them, I was so full of gratitude I had tears in my eyes. These are the folks who match their words with actions. Who amplifies the voice of the voiceless. They're the ones who always have our backs and keep us going.

The PCPC delivered the exact same message as before, but through a different representative: a lawyer from a big DC law firm

I'll never be able to adequately thank everyone who came out to support SB 1249. They helped save millions of animals.

From left to right: Katie Cleary, Harley Quinn Smith, Senator Cathleen Galgiani, Maggie Q, me, and Senator Toni Atkins.

Me, Senator Galgiani, and Hilary Pickles of Lush testifying at the Assembly Judiciary Committee hearing for SB 1249.

who had flown in for the hearing. Listening to her, you'd think cosmetic manufacturers were the most ethical companies in the world. She said her clients were talking to regulators in China to get them to accept nonanimal testing, they just needed more time. They always need just a little more time. According to her, our bill could create trade barriers, incentivize companies to offshore manufacturing to China, and might even eliminate entire categories of personal care products. In the apocalyptic world she described, you could imagine Californians one day walking around with greasy hair because shampoo was banned, smelling up every space they entered because deodorant couldn't be found in stores, and losing all their teeth because toothpaste was illegal.

The representative from the California Manufacturers' and Technology Association labeled SB 1249 a "manufacturing breaker." They had the same handful of witnesses in opposition.

We breathed a sigh of relief when the matter was brought back to the dais and Chair Mark Stone reminded everyone that China may be a big market, but so is California. What's the point of having that kind of economic power if we don't use it to effect positive change?

Our point exactly.

In my years of working in politics at the state Capitol, I've become deeply convinced that you can divide politicians into two categories. There are those who are in it for themselves. They get hooked on the power and influence. They love courting contributions, counting money, and getting attention, and that's the only reason they stick around. Others are in it to do good for their districts and humanity. I say humanity because these public servants think about the bigger picture, beyond the issues and desires of those who elected them. Though they certainly work tirelessly for their constituents, they are also willing to take big and bold action that has an impact well outside their districts.

What we were proposing with the cosmetics bill was a positive change that would have a ripple effect worldwide. Something that went way beyond petty political rivalries and ego-driven ambitions.

Assemblymember Ash Kalra of San Jose is in politics for the right reasons. He's a true animal rights and human rights champion, an outspoken vegan, and one of SCIL's closest allies. Everything he does is to improve the lives of animals, people, and the planet. A former public defender, Assemblymember Kalra has taken those skills and credentials and expanded them in the legislature. Basically, he's defending all of us—those who have a voice and those who don't—and always speaking from the heart. That day, during the Judiciary Committee hearing, Assemblymember Kalra, a joint coauthor of SB 1249, introduced the personal side of the argument. People use cosmetics to look good so they can feel good. How can you feel good knowing the products you buy cause immense suffering? You can't. It's that simple.

Then-Republican Assemblymember Brian Maienschein, who has since switched parties, talked about being a single dad to two teenage girls, and how shopping for cosmetics with them had opened his eyes to the issue. He and his daughters looked for the cruelty-free label because in so doing, they knew they were saving animals and sparing them from torture.

It was a powerful moment. You can feel the mood shift when lawmakers start sharing personal stories about why they support your bill, especially if you know their political party has instructed them to vote against it. Such a big part of our work is to get politicians to see the real-world impacts of the bills they're considering. There's no satisfaction like watching them come around.

But politicians also have to be careful to not interfere with business. The opposition's voice was louder than ours on this front. Lawmakers were especially worried about the sunset of the China exception and the prospect of ingredients being banned because they were tested for non-cosmetic purposes. As the other side pointed out, some makers of personal care products have divisions that manufacture cleaning products, and may have ingredients they use for both lines, including scents. The law could put them at a disadvantage to companies that don't have multi-sector lines.

During the back and forth with the committee members, one of the anti-SB 1249 witnesses drove home that the Chinese cosmetic market is bigger than California's. She warned the members: Don't make companies choose. Because they'll go where the money is.

That was the opposition's main message and the committee heard it.

I did my best to respond. All these questions had been hashed out during the debate on the EU rule. Cosmetic makers had fear-mongered about jobs there too, but the rule ended up sparking a boom in the European tech industry as companies offering nonanimal testing alternatives proliferated. Jobs grew.

JPMS used a nonanimal test conducted by a Boston-based company that Chinese regulators accepted. Multinational cosmetic companies had five years to follow a path that had already been created for them. Not to mention that the rule only applied to physical stores. They were free to sell online in China through Alibaba, the world's largest e-commerce site. Hong Kong had its own rules about what could be sold in brick-and-mortar stores, so there was no barrier there.

The opposition wouldn't let it go. They wanted the same China carve-out as in the EU rule.

Senator Galgiani insisted that we had already taken three major amendments and given them the carve-out, but with a sunset. It was more than reasonable. China would follow our lead and evolve by 2023.

We're California. We don't volunteer to stay behind because others refuse to move forward. We blaze the trail.

By the time the hearing was over, we knew the committee members understood that the EU's carve-out for China had created a gaping loophole that was being exploited by manufacturers. They knew California could close it, and possibly go even further. But we weren't sure if they were ready to do it. Senator Galgiani said she'd continue to work with both sides and find a compromise everyone could agree on.

The bill passed out of committee on a resounding 9-to-0 vote, but there were apprehensions.

■ ■ ■

On July 2, we added yet another exemption. As the opposition brought up repeatedly, some ingredients are tested for use in non-cosmetic products, and our bill would have made it illegal to use those same components in cosmetics. So we amended the bill to allow those ingredients to be used, but under one condition: the animal testing had to be required by a government agency, and the ingredient had to be already in cosmetic use for at least one year. Also, the testing had to be conducted by a firm not associated with the cosmetic manufacturer. Our goal was to prevent situations where companies said they were testing for non-cosmetic purposes but then started using the ingredients in cosmetic products.

It was a concession, but one that preserved our intent.

PETA brought the science to the SB 1249 fight—and brought the rat to the press conference.

Assemblymember Ash Kalra spoke from the heart at our press conference. Directly behind him are me and Elizabeth Baker. Behind us are Nick Sackett, Gloria Butler, Lisa Karlin, and Patty Shenker.

A few days before the bill went to Assembly Appropriations on August 8, we made one more minor technical amendment, granting some exemptions for tests required by a government agency for drug development.

For about a week running up to the vote, we plastered the city with billboards showing bunnies being tortured in labs. They were graphic and real and in everyone's faces. The message was the same on every one: YES ON SB 1249. Dr. Michelson, PCRM, PETA, and small donors helped fund that campaign with generous contributions. It was effective. We created a buzz and added a wow factor. We sent the message that there was money and juice behind the campaign, that this was a serious issue people had better take seriously.

Our success was narrower in the Appropriations Committee. The bill made it out with eleven ayes and six noes, but we knew we were heading in the right direction because the governor's office started pinging us to iron out details. The administration saw that SB 1249 would soon be landing on Governor Jerry Brown's desk and wanted to pave the way for it to become law.

A few weeks before the August 31 Assembly floor vote, we took over the West Steps and lawn of the Capitol building for a major press conference. PETA and PCRM were instrumental in making the event so successful. Lush was there handing out swag; Ben & Jerry's served up vegan ice cream. We had food stands, celebrities including Alicia Silverstone, Jane Velez-Mitchell, and Katie Cleary mixing and mingling, and a DJ spinning tunes. Basically, we created our own little city right there on the lawn. Legislators and staffers stopped by to grab a bite and listen to a song and be reminded that there was only one right way to vote.

Meanwhile, behind closed doors, a high-level staff member from the governor's office was talking to a big animal rights group, one that hadn't put in any of the effort but wanted to get all the kudos. Governor Brown was nearing the end of his second term, so everyone who worked for him knew they'd have to find other jobs soon. In such situations, staffers are often offered lucrative positions with lobbying and public affairs firms eager to leverage the relationships they've established while in government. Their insider status is so much more valuable to the companies they join than any amount of money they could be paid.

A little favor can go a long way in politics. Big favors can land big opportunities.

Our lobbying team checking in with Assemblymember Ash Kalra.

I organized a special appreciation lunch at Ella for John Salley, Dr. Michael Klapper, and others who had traveled to town to lobby for SB 1249.

NBA Champion John Salley came to the Capitol to support the California Cruelty-Free Cosmetics Act. Shown here having some fun with me and Assemblymember Brian Maienschein, whose basketball John signed.

Dr. Michelson had been warning me that someone on the governor's staff might be eyeing a career move into the lobbying industry. Over and over again, he reminded me to brace for a last-minute backroom deal as people—both elected officials and those who work for them—focused more on their own futures than on carrying out their duties.

We also knew that other animal rights groups were very jealous that we were getting so close to getting this done, and we were anticipating maneuvers from them as well.

I shouldn't have been surprised when I walked into a meeting called by the governor's office to see, seated comfortably and waiting for me, a top official from one of the animal rights groups that had been working to get its fingerprints on the bill, along with one of their lobbyists. The governor's office was going to require one last amendment to get the bill signed. The other group had already promised to support it, which only increased the pressure on us to take the amendment. It also gave the other group the cover it needed to associate its name with a new law on which it was a late follower, not a leader.

It wasn't the first time I'd found myself in such a situation, and it won't be the last. But that day I was particularly disgusted. Was there no bottom to the sliminess of these people? This bill would save millions of animal lives. And one of the biggest and wealthiest animal groups in the country was trying to water down the protections we wanted to secure for the animals, just to bolster its own credentials and fundraise off our success.

This last amendment was all the justification this group needed to take full credit for getting the bill passed. I still feel the pit in my stomach when I picture its email blast in my inbox: "We did it! We banned products tested on animal products in California!"

After watching SCIL, PCRM, PETA, and Dr. Michelson do all the work, they were calling the victory their own.

As Dr. Michelson predicted, the staffer from the governor's office who brought the other group into the conversation at the last minute now works as a lobbyist. One of her firm's clients is a health tech company that tests on animals.

After endless back and forth with the governor's office, we took the final major amendments on August 28, just days before the Assembly floor vote. In the end, we carved out an exemption for animal-tested ingredients and products if testing was done outside the manufacturer's supply chain. And we took out the China exemption sunset. It just wasn't going to make it through with that five-year deadline looming, as the governor's staff had made clear.

Knowing that might happen, we had a backup plan: In its final iteration, the bill specified that substantiating safety data accepted in California could not be derived from animal tests. In other words, companies were free to conduct animal tests to get into the Chinese market, under the pretext that they had no choice, but they couldn't use data *derived from those tests* to sell in California. Rather, they'd have to provide separate, nonanimal tests.

Ethically and financially, cosmetic companies were thus much better off going cruelty-free and working to get China to accept non-animal tests. That was the new incentive structure our bill created.

With SB 1249 now essentially in line with the EU rule, lawmakers had no reason to oppose it anymore. Their concerns had been addressed in a way that preserved most of our intent and definitely represented progress. On August 31, 2018, the bill passed the Assembly unanimously. After a quick trip back to the Senate for a concurrence vote (39-to-0 with one member not recording a vote), it headed to the governor's desk.

In September, when Governor Brown signed SB 1249 into law, he officially made California the first state in the nation to ban the sale of cosmetics or personal hygiene products if the final product or any component of it was tested on animals, effective January 1, 2020, with limited exceptions for regulatory requirements.

The world's fifth-largest economy was sending a clear message to companies: history is moving in the direction of protecting animals. Get on board or get left behind.

It didn't take long to see results.

Several of the multinationals that fought us tooth and nail changed their tune right away. Overnight, I started seeing commercials for shampoos and soaps that had been around forever suddenly touting their cruelty-free creds.

If they got anything out of this fight, they learned that the consumers they needed to appeal to were on our side. Those companies might not care about animals, but they do care about their sales.

As we had predicted, other states followed California's lead. Nevada and Illinois in 2019. Virginia, Maryland, Maine, Hawaii and New Jersey in 2021. Louisiana and New York in 2022. In 2023, Oregon brought the total to eleven.

As I write, over forty countries have banned or placed limitations on cosmetic animal testing. In 2021, Mexico became the first North American country to outlaw cosmetic testing on animals. The Organization for Economic Cooperation and Development (OECD) has approved new nonanimal test guidelines.

In March 2021, the Chinese government announced that it would allow companies to import and sell general cosmetics in stores with no pre-market animal testing required. Note that it didn't completely reverse its earlier policy. Animal testing is still required for "special" cosmetics, and companies still have hoops to jump through to get their products into China. But if they're selling makeup, shampoos, nail polish, lotions or other ordinary cosmetics, they have no excuse not to take those steps.

In January 2023, China eliminated the requirement for post-market animal testing.

When I say that our bill shook up the global economy, and saved animals exponentially, this is what I mean.

Just as we launched our partnership with PCRM by looking at what had been done in other countries, you can be sure that other states and countries were looking to California's example after SB 1249 passed. It's exactly how we like to operate. Building on the success of those who came before us, we introduce groundbreaking laws that serve as a model for others to make the world more humane and safer for animals.

CHAPTER 13

MAKING HISTORY, AGAIN AND AGAIN

The paradigm shift in lawmakers' attitudes toward animal bills was a long time in the making. SCIL's willingness to tackle issues when others said it was too soon helped. So did our relentless work to put a spotlight on voting records. For too many years, voters went to the polls with no idea where candidates stood on animal issues. There was no incentive for those seeking office to talk about the subject on the campaign trail. Once elected, legislators could get by for years without ever taking a stand or voting on a single bill related to animals.

Our messaging at SCIL focused not only on the bills making their way through the legislature, but also on who was voting on them—or not voting. We'd encourage people to contact their legislators. To let assemblymembers A, B, and C know that they should support a certain Assembly bill, to tell senators X, Y, and Z to vote no on a specific Senate bill.

There is no way to force legislators to do their job every time. Lord knows too many of them sit on their hands when they're supposed to be voting. We keep track of that too. Draw attention to their courage, or lack thereof. Remind them that not voting sends just as strong a message as pushing the yes or no button.

With the bills we were sponsoring, hiding in the shadows became more problematic. Starting in 2007, we created a conversation at the state level about pet overpopulation and California's shameful euthanasia rates. Ten years later, our sponsored bill banning mill-bred animals from pet stores helped tackle that problem in a brand-new way. Passed at exactly the right time (despite what our detractors said), it sent a clear message that what was once considered extreme was now doable.

As 2018 wound down, our groundbreaking cosmetics bill continued to make headlines across the country and around the world. Lawmakers who backed it were rightly seen as bold and were basking in the praise.

For the first time, there was even a financial upside to getting on the right side of animal issues. We'd played a part in that as well. Our deep-pocketed opponents had spent money like there was no tomorrow to defeat us. They had an endless supply of it. My main lobbyist on the bill reminded me that while we'd never be able to keep up with those big companies financially, we had something else of great value: our close relationships with some very influential donors in Southern California. People who could make substantial contributions to campaigns and who lawmakers would definitely like to meet.

After the success of the cosmetics bill, we decided to leverage the power of those connections by putting on a fundraising luncheon no one would forget. It took a while to find a venue that

Nick Sackett, Erika Brunson, me, Crystal Moreland, Margie Perenchio, and Katie Cleary after a day of meeting with animal-friendly legislators.

would prepare vegan food and could seat everyone we planned to invite. Not an easy task, given how many of the large dining spaces in Sacramento are steakhouses inside hotels. I arranged for a private room at Echo & Rig and worked with the chef to create an entirely plant-based menu.

Every assemblymember and senator who had supported us or been a friend was invited. So were people who had leaned in our direction or lent a hand.

We spent weeks going over the guest list and deciding how much we were going to give to each politician. The total campaign contributions to all candidates combined came to about $165,000. Margie Perenchio and Erika Brunson—now in their twelfth year supporting SCIL—each committed to cover a third of the total. Dr. Michelson donated the rest. Margie and Erika flew up from Bel-Air on a private jet. They were elated to have the opportunity to meet one-on-one with lawmakers and speak directly with them about how important it was to protect animals and how it should be a bipartisan issue.

It was a first-of-its-kind event that would forever be associated with the name SCIL. As would the campaign contributions made that day. I had learned, begrudgingly, lessons about branding. Networking. Relational lobbying. Call it what you will; it does have an impact.

One state senator, a real animal lover who'd long been an ally of ours and has carried major bills for us, pulled me aside afterward. He said, "Judie, people will be talking about this luncheon for years. I've never seen another group have an event like this in such a transparent way. Well done."

He was right about our forthright approach being unprecedented. Lobbyists usually bundle money from clients or deliver it for them. They might arrange for a quick conversation out of the spotlight, one that includes mention of a contribution that has been made or could be forthcoming from a client.

With us, there was no question about who was getting contributions or where they were coming from.

Our lobbyists' minds were blown too. They'd never seen anything like it. Those not invited that day heard about it, and were paying attention too. Suddenly SCIL wasn't some little animal rights group coming around with a tin cup. We were out in front, making things happen, leading the way, and bringing others along with us.

After years of struggling to get our name out there and educate the public about our work, we had people reaching out to see how they could help. Lawmakers who in the past would literally turn and run the other way when they saw me coming were now making a beeline for me when I was in the Capitol, saying, "If you have a good animal bill that needs an author, I'm here."

It was truly the dawn of a new era. Nick and I could feel it. And we knew we had to strike while the iron was hot.

■ ■ ■

So we dove into 2019 feet first, sponsoring as many bills as we could effectively manage.

But first, a celebration. Another event, right on the heels of our luncheon. To acknowledge everything we'd accomplished in 2018 and properly thank everyone who'd contributed to our incredible successes.

On January 19, our "Sunset on Sunset" event kicked off at 4:30 p.m. at the Andaz West Hollywood hotel, on the world-famous Sunset Strip, one of my main stomping grounds when I moved to Hollywood in the 1980s as a music lover. Growing up in Missouri, I went to every concert I could. In St. Louis, that meant mostly stadium shows or hole-in-the-wall clubs. As soon as we were old enough to drive, my friends and I would make weekly treks to Chicago to check out the hottest venues.

LA in the late 1980s was heaven for someone like me. Where else could I hear so many soon-to-be-world-famous bands play small venues? The Sunset Strip was the ultimate destination for that. And the clubs near Andaz were some of my favorite haunts.

I'm not saying we felt like rock stars when we booked the Andaz for our fundraiser, but we sure were proud of the waves we were making and looking forward to more big wins.

With floor-to-ceiling windows offering sweeping views of the Los Angeles skyline and Pacific Ocean, the Panorama Ballroom was ours for the evening. Jane Velez-Mitchell acted as emcee with Lisa Bloom, a renowned civil rights attorney, animal rights activist, and

Me with honorees Assemblymember Ash Kalra, John Paul DeJoria, and Assemblymember Adrin Nazarian. The Tenth, Harley Quinn Smith's band, performing behind us.

committed vegan since 2009. City Councilmember Paul Koretz was on hand to present John Paul DeJoria with an official proclamation from the City of Los Angeles for his philanthropic work and advocacy for anti-cruelty laws. SCIL honored him as well, of course. John Paul was so instrumental in passing the cosmetics bill, the event wouldn't have been complete without him.

Elected officials showed up in force, including city councilmembers and state representatives. We honored Senator Nancy Skinner for the vanguard legislation she authored to get plant-based meals into state hospitals and prisons.

Never before had we had so many politicians go out of their way to attend one of our fundraisers. Nick told me afterward that for the first time, it felt like SCIL was the group to watch, and our events were the place to be.

There certainly was something in the air.

Our newfound popularity wasn't limited to politicians. Success breeds success at different levels, as we were discovering every day. Our honorees that night included Maggie Q and youth climate and animal rights activist Genesis Butler, a.k.a. the Amazing Animal Ally. Genesis was one of the youngest people ever to give a TED Talk at the age of ten. Just twelve years old when she attended our event, Genesis was already a powerful leader in the animal rights space. Maggie Q would join the SCIL board in June, along with Hollywood legend Diane Keaton. Diane knew our longtime supporter Margie Perenchio through a neighborhood group that got together regularly for movie nights. During one such event, Margie talked to Diane about animal rights, and told her about SCIL. Before you knew it, Diane and I were on the phone discussing all the projects we had in the pipeline, and she was accepting a position on our board. Rarely have I met a star who's as gracious and generous with her time as Diane Keaton. She spends time talking to everyone at every event she attends.

Genesis became our newest and youngest-ever board member in 2021.

Our growing star power was, and is, helping us create a solid bridge with the next generation of activists and leaders.

We also gave awards that night to Joanna Krupa, actor, model, animal activist, and businesswoman, and to Linda Middlesworth, who went vegan after being diagnosed with heart disease and thyroid cancer on the eve of her forty-fifth birthday and inspired others to follow. Now approaching eighty, she's still thriving and educating others about how plant-based living can heal.

Another big announcement we made that night: after being subject to delayed implementation to give stores more time to adjust to the new business model, our puppy mill bill was finally taking effect. California consumers would no longer be able to buy dogs, cats, or rabbits from commercial or backyard breeders in pet stores. Only rescue and shelter animals would be available for adoption. The law was being copied in other states too.

Making waves across the country and around the world. Nowhere else we'd rather be.

The mood was one of joy and excitement. Enthusiasm about our future was at its peak. Once the awards were done, actor and activist Harley Quinn Smith treated us to an evening of fantastic music with her punk band The Tenth.

We celebrated and danced the night away, knowing that the next morning, we'd roll up our sleeves and dive into our busiest year yet.

■ ■ ■

The deadline for introducing new bills in 2019 was February 22. We were ahead of the game with a few pieces of sponsored legislation. Senate Bill 64 would have mandated microchipping for all reclaimed or adopted pets leaving animal shelters. Just 15 percent of the dogs and 2 percent of the cats brought to shelters without identification ever get reunited with their families. Most of the others wind up being euthanized. These are healthy, adoptable pets that get killed because the shelters don't have their owners' contact information.

Microchipping was a key component of the solution to this unconscionable problem.

Our microchip bill was mostly ready to go, since we'd sponsored a different version of it back in 2011, authored by now-Congressman Ted Lieu. The new version was introduced on January 7 and made it all the way through both houses without a single no vote. What should have been a slam dunk got sidetracked, however, when the powerful association representing the directors of the state's animal control agencies raised concerns about the potential for additional work and the cost of providing the microchips. They were calling it an unfunded mandate.

Sometimes there is a real lack of funding for an initiative and it needs to be addressed. At other times, "unfunded mandate" is code for when an agency or organization doesn't want a bill to pass and knows that raising fears about money is the best way to stop it.

In this case, the argument didn't hold water. Shelters were overcrowded and most of the animals they took in couldn't be identified. Oftentimes, the same animals were brought in again and again. The shelters—and through them the taxpayers—bore the cost of housing those animals and trying to track down their families. Finding them a new home or euthanizing them if they weren't adopted out or reclaimed also cost money.

Yet here we were, quibbling over microchips that could be procured for as little as four dollars apiece.

We agreed to give the shelters an out, saying they could tack the microchip cost onto the fee when families came to reclaim their animals. Even that got pushback. What if the families couldn't afford the extra four dollars?

Everyone agreed that microchips were good policy, but irrational fears about costs ended up winning the day. I've seen this more times than I can count. If you want to tank a bill, start fearmongering about money, even if there's no basis in reality. Such concerns are given so much weight, they can sink even the most straightforward bill.

The animals always pay the price.

In his veto message, Governor Gavin Newsom talked about the perceived burden "on those who may already be struggling with the basic cost of caring for their pets." It was suggested that the bill be reintroduced with an exemption for shelters that said they couldn't cover the cost. So in 2020, we sponsored a revised microchipping bill, Senate Bill 573, authored by Senator Ling Ling Chang. It sailed through both houses and was approved by the governor in September.

Today, every animal released from a public shelter or animal control agency, whether it's being reclaimed by its family or adopted out, is microchipped, with exceptions only if capabilities aren't available on-site or if the animal owners prove that it would be an economic hardship.

It really pained me to carve out all these exemptions and give everybody an excuse not to help solve the pet overpopulation crisis. Especially the shelters, which knew how much of a difference microchips would make. But the bottom line is that we got it done. Making incremental progress is better than standing still. Laws with too many exceptions are better than no laws.

There's no way to know how many animal lives—and taxpayer dollars—that bill saved. All I know for certain is that it has made a big difference.

■ ■ ■

Two other SCIL-sponsored bills made it through both houses in 2019 without a single no vote, only to die on the governor's desk. It's an aspect of legislative advocacy you never get used to. Really good, popular proposals get shot down due to unfounded fears. Assembly Bill 733, authored by Bill Quirk and cosponsored by SCIL and PCRM, would have required the California Department of Toxic Substances Control (DTSC) to stop using an outdated aquatic toxicity test to determine if products should be classified as hazardous waste. Often called the "minnow test," the barbaric process involves dumping waste at different concentrations into a tank with at least forty live fish, either fathead minnows, rainbow trout, or golden shiners. Whatever concentration causes half the fish to die within ninety-six hours is deemed hazardous.

If the results are inconclusive, the test is repeated. Over and over again. Killing more fish every time.

There are so many problems with this it's hard to know where to begin. Top of mind for animal rights activists and ethical scientists is that fish are sentient beings. Science leaves no doubt about this. When people think about animal tests, they often picture rabbits, mice, rats, even dogs and monkeys. Not fish. Today, a growing number of people, companies and government agencies are acknowledging the sentience of our aquatic friends and speaking out against disgusting practices like fish kill tests.

Then there is the inaccuracy of the tests. Fish can die due to causes other than toxicity. For instance, the cosmetic product, pesticide, or other substance being tested might get in their gills and cause them to suffocate. With these tests, the cause of death doesn't matter. All DTSC looks at is how many fish die and how many hours it takes. In other words, fish are subjected to abject cruelty for results that might not even reflect toxicity when humane alternatives exist.

We'd sponsored a first version of the bill in 2018 but it was vetoed despite broad agreement that California should adopt twenty-first century methods. AB 733 would force DTSC to make the transition to humane alternatives.

No big deal. Unquestionably the right thing to do.

We even had the Personal Care Products Council on our side, for the first and maybe the last time. Remember, that's one of the main groups that fought us tooth and nail on the animal-tested cosmetics bill a year earlier. After we won that battle, more consumer product makers than ever started taking the cruelty-free pledge. It was in those brands' interest to go on the record opposing tests that killed fish.

They had an economic incentive too. If makers of personal care products wanted to be considered cruelty-free, the simplest way was to label all the waste produced by their manufacturing processes as toxic. That way, there's no testing and categorizing to be done. Many chose that route. As a result, waste from the production of everyday items like nearly all soaps and shampoos was automatically classified as hazardous, even if it wasn't. Companies were paying more to treat it for no good reason. Not to mention that hazardous waste can't be recycled—it can only be incinerated. So keeping the outdated aquatic test as the standard in California was bad for the environment too.

Governor Newsom's veto message focused on DTSC being underfunded. Fearmongering about money worked once again, sadly. When an agency or department says it doesn't have the funds to do something, the governor has to take it seriously. Even when the real problem is that an agency or department simply doesn't want to change its ways.

After the veto, we agreed with PCRM that we should work directly with DTSC to find a way for it to leave this awful test behind.

We hired a lobbyist who had worked for Assemblymember Quirk before. Over the next two years, he helped us find funding for DTSC to explore alternative test methods.

During that time, two other versions of the bill failed to get through the legislature.

Once again, the third time was the charm. Assemblymember Quirk brought a new version back in 2022, AB 1793, sponsored this time by the National Stewardship Action Council, with the Personal Care Products Council listed as registered support. Rather than focusing on the cruelty of the tests, the author looked at the problem from the recycling angle. If a calculation-based method could measure hazardousness as effectively as fish kill tests, then more companies would use it, avoiding that much unnecessary incineration. Products found not to be hazardous could be donated or reused rather than burned. Everybody came out ahead.

AB 1793 sailed through both houses with no opposition, as had happened with the version we sponsored. This time, the governor signed it into law.

■ ■ ■

Depressingly, SCIL-sponsored Senate Bill 202 was also vetoed after getting nothing but aye votes throughout the legislative process. Known as the "doggy donor bill," it was a response to the chronic shortage of blood products veterinarians faced throughout the state. Hard as it is to believe, in 2019, California was the only state in the nation where vets who needed blood products for surgeries had to draw it themselves, at their own practice, or purchase it from closed-colony blood banks.

Closed-colony refers to facilities where dogs and cats are kept on-site, in cages, for months or even years on end, so their blood can be drawn repeatedly. These animals are known as "blood slaves."

Former racing greyhounds are the donors of choice since they're likely to have a universal blood type. Those poor dogs go from being abused and exploited at racetracks to living in cramped cages and getting their blood drawn every ten days or so for commercial purposes for years on end. They're sent from one inhumane situation to another when a perfectly good alternative exists: community blood banks, where animals can be brought in to give blood and then taken home afterward, similar to the way Red Cross centers work for humans.

Because of California's restrictive and outdated laws on animal blood donation, the only two commercially licensed blood banks in the state were closed-colony. The University of California Davis veterinary school had been operating a community blood bank since 2008, but it was prohibited by law from selling blood it drew to other veterinary clinics.

The bill we sponsored in 2019 would simply have allowed the California Department of Food and Agriculture (CDFA) to license other community blood banks so they could get up and running in the state and eventually compete with, then replace, closed-colony facilities. Unfortunately, some overly zealous activists convinced the governor that because the bill didn't go far enough to shut down the closed-colony banks right away, it deserved to be vetoed. And that's what happened.

Refusing to take a step forward because it seems too small is the exact opposite of how SCIL likes to proceed. We're activists at heart and would love to change everything all at once to save all the animals. Believe me, we would if we could. But we have to be practical. Reasonable. Take what we can get and come back later for more.

Once again, our work was not lost. Inspired by and based on our text, two more bills aimed at shutting down closed-colony banks were introduced the following year. Neither made it through committees, but in 2021, the authors teamed up to jointly introduce Assembly Bill 1282, the California Pet Blood Bank Modernization Act. It allows commercial blood banks to produce blood from community-sourced donor animals, much like the human donor model, and will eventually phase out the closed-colony production model for dogs. In addition, it adds more transparency and oversight regarding how animal blood banks are run in California. Some outdated provisions in our laws allowed closed-colony facilities to operate without providing any information to the public about how donor animals were treated. AB 1282 changed that and put the state on a path toward a humane model.

Happily, not all our bills had to follow such a circuitous route to become law. Three pieces of landmark legislation that we sponsored made it through the legislature and got the governor's signature in 2019. Right away, they began changing the landscape for animals, and animal exploiters, in California and beyond.

■ ■ ■

Ending fur trapping had been a dream of mine since 2013, when the legislature adopted Assembly Bill 1213 prohibiting the trapping of bobcats in areas around state parks and wildlife refuges.

Known as the Bobcat Protection Act, AB 1213 was introduced after a conservationist found a trap illegally set on his property near Joshua Tree National Park. The cats were protected inside state parks, but around the edges they were fair game.

It quickly came to light that trappers were scanning wildlife lovers' social media feeds to track bobcat sightings then setting their traps in those areas.

Bobcats are beautiful animals that are vital to our ecosystem. A small group of trappers engaging in a practice from another century was steadily chipping away at the population, especially with demand from China and Russia driving up the price of pelts and making their business much more lucrative.

The Bobcat Protection Act directed the California Fish and Game Commission to establish trapping-free buffer zones around areas where trapping was already prohibited. But two years after it went into law, little had changed. Inhumane traps continued to be set, and bobcats were being killed with little or no oversight. According to the Bobcat Protection Act, the fees trappers paid for permits to legally trap bobcats needed to cover the full cost of regulating their activities, which added up to hundreds of thousands of dollars a year. Permit fees weren't anywhere close to covering them, meaning monies being allocated to regulation were coming from taxpayers.

The unfunded mandate argument worked in our favor for once. No one could argue that the state should be subsidizing fur trappers.

In August 2015, the Fish and Game Commission was scheduled to vote on how to best implement the Bobcat Protection Act and what the exact boundaries of the buffer zones should be. Option 1 would ban bobcat trapping in about half the state. Option 2 would essentially turn the whole state into a buffer zone, effectively ending bobcat trapping in California.

No way was I going to sit on the sidelines of this fight.

To bolster support for Option 2 ahead of the August 5 vote, SCIL launched a Ban the Trap billboard and social media campaign across the state, urging Fish and Game and Governor Jerry Brown to end this barbaric practice. Pulling that campaign together was an epic adventure. A lot of people don't know what a bobcat looks like. Well, on those billboards, we showed them a cat in a cage, looking terrified, since that was the reality.

Bringing together all the busy and famous people who'd agreed to pose for the billboard photo was more complicated. Diane Warren, Oscar and Grammy winner for her extraordinary songwriting, offered the deck of her oceanfront Malibu home as a backdrop. Next, we needed to find a time that worked for Dr. Jenn from *Couples Therapy* (who Simone talked into joining us), Katie Cleary and her then-boyfriend Matt Raimo, Gloria Butler, music manager and wife of Black Sabbath's Geezer Butler, as well as *Baywatch* actor Alexandra Paul, me, and Simone Reyes.

Once we were assembled, it took most of the day for the photographer to get the perfect shot. Especially as Diane has a tendency to raise her middle finger at the camera at the very last minute. Every time she pulled that signature move, we'd have to start over. We all wore #BanTheTrap T-shirts for the shoot and donned them again for the major press conference we held the day the billboards went up. Those billboards were the talk of the town and in the news every day. Fish and Game commissioners were seeing them too, everywhere they went. Their offices were getting inundated with phone calls, emails, and letters from people speaking up for the bobcats.

Awareness can be our most powerful tool. Once people learned what bobcat trapping was about, they took action.

Putting the problem in people's faces works.

The Fish and Game meeting was going to be held over two days, August 4 and 5, 2015, in Fortuna, California. I knew I had to be there in person. Katie Cleary and I flew to San Jose and rented a car to continue the journey. What should have been a six-hour drive turned into a two-day trek. Wildfires were raging across California that year. Trinity National Forest was engulfed in flames. The farther north we got, the more roads were blocked off. At one point, a detour led us deep into a forest. We had no idea where we were headed. Terrified that the fire might be right behind us, we kept moving forward until we saw flashing signs warning us to TURN AROUND. We had been driving straight into the fire!

Once out of the danger zone, we started looking for a place to get a few hours of sleep. All the hotel rooms were occupied by people who'd had to evacuate. It was one of the most harrowing experiences I've ever had. But also an awe-inspiring one. I'd never explored as much of California by car as I did during that road trip. Seeing all those majestic landscapes being ravaged by wildfires only increased my determination to save not just our precious wildlife but all the natural environment that makes this state unique.

Even with the detours and extra time spent on the road, the trip was absolutely worth it. Walking into the Commission hearing, we got applause and hugs from animal welfare and environmental groups we'd never heard of. They'd seen the billboards and online ads and thanked us for making a big difference. We were throwing the love right back at them. These were the compassionate Californians who'd made the phone calls, sent the emails, and even battled wildfires to show up for the meeting in person.

Of the over one hundred members of the public who went to the microphone, only a handful were not in support of banning bobcat trapping across the state.

It was at that meeting that I was first introduced to the work of the Center for Biological Diversity, and I became an instant fan. The main presentation was given by Brendan Cummings, the organization's Conservation Director. My mind was blown by his passion, his compassion, his mastery of science—and by CBD's army of

The photo shoot for the billboard: me, Alexandra Paul, Matt Raimo, Katie Cleary, Gloria Butler, and Diane Warren (adding her personal touch). Front, Dr. Jenn Mann and Simone Reyes.

Simone Reyes, Gloria Butler, me, Dr. Jenn Mann, LA City Councilmember Paul Koretz, Dr. Karen Halligan, Katie Cleary, Joey Herrick, Matt Raimo, and Jenn Andrews the day the official #BanTheTrap billboard was unveiled.

supporters. Tens of thousands of people had called in or submitted letters asking the commissioners to vote for Option 2.

Partnering with CBD in 2019, on the fur trapping bill, would be another dream come true.

Ultimately, by a vote of just 3-to-2, the Commission approved a statewide ban on commercial and recreational bobcat trapping. When the vote is as close as that, you can look back and know that every action you took was worth it. Every ounce of pressure you applied helped move the needle.

Years later, a commissioner told me that he had tried to find a road to work that didn't take him by one of our billboards, but he couldn't. How did I know where to place them? My little secret, I said. (I'd simply looked up where their offices were and planned accordingly.)

The ban was the first of its kind in the nation. Once again, California was leading the way. I was thrilled with the outcome, of

Enjoying our sweet success with other bobcat lovers in Fortuna. Left to right, Erin Hauge, Jana Hofeditz, Leah Sturgis, Katie Cleary, me, Camilla Fox, Guy Strahl, and Fauna Tomlinson.

course, but I couldn't shake the feeling that we'd left behind the other species that were still being trapped for their fur. That we needed to go back and protect them all.

■ ■ ■

Late in 2018, I got a call from Dr. Michelson.

"Judie, let's do a fur ban next year."

I looked at our calendar for 2019, how full it was already.

"We've got so many other bills in the pipeline. This would be a tall order. I'm not even sure it's the right time. We'd need to get polling done."

"I'll take care of the polling. You find the author."

Before I knew it, we had a pollster preparing a detailed survey of people's views on a host of animal rights issues. It was a unique opportunity to explore what Californians knew and thought about how our state laws did and didn't protect animals, and how they felt about those protections, particularly when it came to fur trapping and fur sales.

Basically, we were taking the temperature. Residents want to protect animals in general; polling always makes that clear. The challenge is to figure out how far their support goes.

Dr. Michelson found that some of the questions weren't specific enough and rewrote them himself. With his changes, the survey gave us invaluable insights for the work that lay ahead. One thing we knew for certain: the public was in our corner when it came to protecting fur-bearing animals. Massively.

Initially, we wanted to end not just trapping but also fur sales. Assemblymember Lorena Gonzalez, a fierce animal lover and the second most powerful member of the Assembly at the time as

We could not have asked for a stronger author for our fur trapping ban than Assemblymember Lorena Gonzales, who Nick and I dropped in to thank after a successful vote.

Appropriations chair was open to the idea of carrying the bill for us. A state senator was potentially ready to join as a coauthor. Just as we were gearing up to get the bill moving, we learned that a national animal welfare group had found a different assemblymember to author a fur sales ban. This was the same group that had taken credit for the puppy mill bill they spent six months trying to sabotage, then took credit for our cosmetics bill, which it had tried to hijack and claim as its own. I contacted the author immediately and offered to form a coalition. Ideally, I'd want SCIL to take the lead, given our record in California and the momentum we'd built up. If SCIL sponsors a bill, people know we're not going to take amendments unnecessarily or let the legislation get so watered down it doesn't do as much as it could. But I was also open to the idea of just being part of the team.

I was shocked when she said no. We were all on the same side, in theory. Getting the despicable fur trade out of California was our common goal. Wasn't it?

To this day, I'm convinced that we got pushed aside because of our big victories of previous years. Kicking puppy mills out of pet stores when the big national groups said the time wasn't right. Stopping sales of animal-tested cosmetics in California when they said it could never be done—or at least that it couldn't be done by us.

Banning fur sales was a very high-profile undertaking, and the big groups needed a big win. SCIL leading it would have further cemented our image as the organization that was getting the most done for the animals and getting the most attention.

Well, we couldn't include fur sales in our bill when other legislation was being introduced to achieve the same goal. So, not without regret, we let it go and focused solely on fur trapping.

SCIL often goes into battles like this allied with partners. I may be good at politics and coalition-building, but I'm not an expert in every field. Luckily, there are a few groups that have all the necessary expertise and are totally aligned with our values. PCRM has some of the best toxicologists in the world, and its commitment to animal rights is unparalleled. PETA brings science, documentation, data galore, and fearlessness to every fight, as well as more grassroots support across the country than we'll ever have. We've even partnered with the National Resources Defense Council. For Assembly Bill 273, the Wildlife Protection Act of 2019, we teamed up with the Center for Biological Diversity (CBD) as cosponsors, as we had done for the ill-fated Iconic African Species Protection Act in 2018. CBD has deep scientific knowledge, passion, and compassion all in one place. And you'll never find anyone more knowledgeable about California laws regarding wildlife than Brendan Cummings.

AB 273 was introduced on January 14, 2019 and assigned to the Committee on Water, Parks and Wildlife in March. Assemblymember Gonzalez presented the bill, stressing the dangers trapping presented to protected species and pets, and the fact that it was subsidized by taxpayers. A representative for CBD spoke about how a single trapper operating along the boundary of Joshua Tree National Park killed enough bobcats in one season to deplete the local population to such an extent that, five years later, sightings

SCIL got into a good groove with press conferences for big bills.
This one was for our fur trapping ban.

were still rare. In 2018, one trapper hovering near the edges of the recently designated San Gabriel Mountains National Monument killed more than a hundred gray foxes. President Obama had declared the San Gabriel Monument in large part to protect local species there. It didn't stop that trapper from significantly depleting the gray fox population.

The testimony stressed how much these losses matter to all the people who live and recreate in these areas. Healthy wildlife populations are integral to healthy communities and a strong tourism industry. Wildlife viewing contributes an estimated $3.5 billion to the California economy. Ecologically, economically, and ethically, banning fur trapping was the right thing to do.

We had dozens of add-on witnesses. People had come from all over the state to sit in on the hearing and spend a few seconds at the microphone, saying their name and stating their support.

It was an uphill battle for the opposition, though they gave it their best shot. I wouldn't have wanted to be them. Representing the fur industry and hunting lobby in a room full of wildlife lovers? No thanks.

After the Appropriations Committee, which Assemblymember Gonzalez chaired, the bill passed the Assembly floor on April 25 with fifty-one ayes, nineteen noes, and ten members not bothering to vote. By this time, lawmakers had listened to a lot of gut-wrenching testimony. About how coyotes, gray foxes, beavers, badgers, and minks spent hours or days stuck in traps and were then strangled, shot, or beaten to death to avoid damaging their pelts. They were moved by hearing about how gruesome the industry was. How antiquated. And how much it was costing taxpayers. In 2017, some seventy trappers were still operating in California, and they killed more than 1,500 animals collectively. As with bobcat trapping, their license fees were supposed to cover the cost of regulating and overseeing the trapping program, but they didn't come anywhere close.

Without massive public subsidies for this deeply unpopular practice, the industry would be long gone. And long gone is exactly where we wanted it. In her author's statement, Assemblymember Gonzalez called it an "outdated vestige of the Wild West." Time to move into this century, people.

■ ■ ■

Initially, the opposition came from the California Farm Bureau. It said fur trapping was a vital tool for the agricultural community. The story went that farmers and ranchers would let recreational trappers onto their land to do their dirty work, allegedly for free, since the trappers could turn around and sell the pelts. This tool would be lost, according to the Farm Bureau. It was a false narrative. So-called depredation permits would work exactly as they always had. Property

Assembly Water, Parks, and Wildlife Committee, Tuesday, March 12, 2019

California is still the only state in the nation that bans recreational and commercial fur trapping. We're hoping others will follow our lead.

This is the view of the Assembly floor from the balcony, which was for years my home away from home.

owners could still get permits to kill for "pest control" purposes if they said animals were damaging their pets, livestock, or crops. All AB 273 would do is ban the recreational and commercial trapping of more than ten fur-bearing species for money, or for "fun."

The Farm Bureau went from simply arguing that the system worked just fine, nothing to see here, to bringing in every group it could find to oppose the ban. And the claims grew more outlandish. By the time AB 273 made it to the Assembly floor in April, you'd have thought the fur trapping ban would be the end of the world. Here's how they framed it: Farmers and ranchers would lose the only tool at their disposal to control wildlife on their property. The Fish and Wildlife Department's authority would be undermined. Trapping in California was a well-regulated industry governed by science-based rules and designed to maintain the exact right balance of wildlife populations, and we were upsetting that balance. Those animal rights groups were overreacting once again!

Anything to preserve the status quo and keep being able to make a living killing animals.

When the bill went to its first Senate committee hearing in June, it seemed like every animal exploitation group in the state had joined the bandwagon. Outfits with names like the California Houndsmen for Conservation and the Cal-Ore Wetland and Waterfowl Council. A county board of supervisors. Hunting groups. The California Rifle & Pistol Association. Gun groups never miss an opportunity to fundraise off bills designed to protect animals. Different bill, same refrain: today it's your fur traps, tomorrow it'll be your guns! They'd been going after us with this line since the spay and neuter bill back in 2007, and they're still doing it today.

Our opponents' list of complaints about AB 273 had grown too, of course. Now it wasn't just about farmers and ranchers not getting their trapping done for free. What about the skills wildlife damage professionals gain when they start out as recreational trappers? All those skills would be lost! The hunters chimed in of course, as they always do, to tout all the good that came from letting them kill California's wildlife for sport.

We weren't having any of these bogus arguments, and neither was Assemblymember Gonzalez. There's nothing like working with a solid author. The nonsense peddlers never got a chance to gain traction with her in charge. One by one, she refuted their claims and addressed her fellow lawmakers' concerns.

Our fiscal argument was also strong. Permit fees weren't coming anywhere near covering the cost of regulating the industry, as Assemblymember Gonzalez hammered home repeatedly. As a result, taxpayers were subsidizing a violent and antiquated practice.

Compassion ended up winning the day. And mathematics. As CBD made clear, the money the pelts generated from foreign fur companies was well below the value these species held for our ecosystems. The California economy brings in much more money from wildlife viewing than it ever could from trapping fees. Without the ban, a handful of old-fashioned trappers would continue to destroy our wildlife to meet consumer demand for fur in China and Russia.

Nobody could defend that.

With no solid economic argument to stand on, and Californians massively siding with the animals, at one point the opposition seemed to accept reality and stopped putting up too much resistance. AB 273 passed a Senate floor vote in August, and Governor Newsom signed it into law on September 4, 2019. Hallelujah!

■ ■ ■

About six weeks after that, Governor Newsom approved AB 44, the bill we had originally wanted to combine with our trapping law. California was now the first state to ban the manufacture and sale of new fur products.

That one had also been a knock-down, drag-out fight from the start. SCIL was a registered supporter and actively lobbied for the bill. During the Senate Natural Resources and Water Committee hearing in June, I sat next to a young activist friend named Julie, who I'd gotten to know from an earlier bill and had been mentoring through this one. She watched a steady stream of people around her age go up to testify against the bill, and said she didn't understand where they came from.

"They're getting paid to be here," I told her.

Her jaw dropped. Then she frowned like she didn't believe me.

"Mark my word, they're getting paid."

Julie spent the rest of the hearing on her phone, looking into this scandalous idea I had just shared with her. I could tell she wasn't going to let it go.

Sure enough, her relentless detective work paid off: On July 10, the day after my conversation with Julie, an article ran in *The Intercept* titled "Protestors Collect Secret Cash to Oppose Fur Ban in California, Documents Reveal." Following up on the tip from Julie, the outlet had obtained documents showing that several opponents who spoke at that and other hearings were compensated for their testimonies. Julie had sent her contact at *The Intercept* other documents suggesting that some of the students were paid too. According to the article, an activist for an animal rights group (Julie) had found a Facebook ad asking, "Anyone in LA down to make an easy $100 this Tuesday in Sacramento and fight tyranny?" Several students said they were interested, as did Julie. She was sent a contract with a Republican consulting firm outlining what she would have to do to earn $175, "with additional opportunities and bonuses for top performers."

This is the nonsense we have to deal with. A big thank you to Julie for doing the deep dive and exposing those frauds.

CHAPTER 14

LETTING WILD ANIMALS BE WILD

Nobody does more for animal rights than PETA. Long before I founded SCIL and started working full-time for the animals, I learned so much—and got so much of my motivation—from reading their writings and watching their videos. Seeing PETA's undercover investigations of factory farms and slaughterhouses with your own eyes will change you forever. I can't tell you how many people I've met who swore off meat and dairy immediately after viewing those videos.

My own history with PETA started sometime in the late 1990s, when an animal activist had me watch one of their videos showing beautiful elephants from the Ringling Bros. circus being beaten, whipped, and hooked. To this day, it's etched in my memory. The look on the animals' faces. The gut-wrenching sounds they were making. You could sense the pain they were experiencing.

Circus operators would go to any lengths to hide what went on behind the scenes. PETA brought it out into the open.

I personally have never been to a circus in my life. It simply wasn't an activity my family participated in when I was growing up. Not for any ethical reasons or anything. Circuses just weren't on our radar. So when I saw that PETA undercover video, I had no personal memories of or connection to the circus experience. All I knew was that those abusers shouldn't be allowed anywhere near animals. Never in my wildest dreams did I imagine that twenty years later, I'd be working side-by-side with PETA to advance animal rights. Yet that's exactly what happened in 2019, when SCIL and PETA cosponsored the Circus Cruelty Prevention Act, Senate Bill 313.

People were waking up to the abject cruelty circus animals experience. They were understanding that in a civilized society, entertainment shouldn't involve exploitation and abuse. Rhode Island banned the use of bullhooks in 2016. Illinois and New York passed laws against using elephants in circuses in 2017. In 2018, I saw a Google alert about New Jersey becoming the first state in the nation to ban wild animals in circus acts.

The New Jersey legislation was called "Nosey's Law." Nosey was a thirty-six-year-old African elephant who was dragged from state to state with a small traveling circus to perform for crowds. Beaten, underfed, and neglected, she spent most of her time in a confined space, in chains, standing in her own excrement. She suffered from severe arthritis, which can be fatal for elephants. Yet she continued to be forced to perform tricks and walk around carrying people on her back. Activists had been working for years to free Nosey, who'd come to be known as the "world's saddest elephant."

The reality is that all animals who get dragged around in cages and used for entertainment live sad and totally unnatural lives.

Toward the end of 2018, SCIL was already talking to lawmakers about authoring a bill banning the transportation of wild animals when we got news that Hawaii had become the second state to outlaw traveling exhibitions with wild animals. The time to act had come.

Once again, we'd have the best partner imaginable. PETA had been working for decades to raise awareness about the cruelty and abuse built into the business model of traveling animal acts. Its activism directly contributed to Ringling Bros. and Barnum & Bailey Circus being shut down in 2017. For years, PETA made sure that when spectators bought tickets, they knew the kind of exploitation and abuse they were supporting. Attendance dropped so low that the owners opted to shut down the whole operation after 146 years in business.

Ben Hueso, a state senator from San Diego, agreed to carry the bill for us. After helping us secure the final votes we needed to get the cosmetics bill off the Senate floor the prior year, he let me know that if we had a good animal bill in need of an author, he'd consider it. We were thrilled to approach him about this, especially as his staff were very pro-animal. There's so much back and forth with staff on bills like this. Having allies throughout the office makes everything flow more easily when an issue is even the least bit controversial. And stopping animals being used for entertainment by traveling acts was very controversial.

■ ■ ■

As initially introduced, our bill would have banned all animals in performances and traveling acts. It would have meant the end of things like roadside and petting zoos, and all those companies that dragged captive animals around to make money would have had to find a different source of income.

If you think it's not fair to shut someone's business down, let's talk about what happens to the animals. How they spend their lives getting hauled around from place to place. Going every day into a different space that's busy and noisy and terrifying for them. All day long, they have people walking up to them, touching them. There's no home to go to at night to recover and relax, to sleep properly and decompress. They're always on the road, either in a small cage or in brand-new surroundings, often undernourished and underhydrated and receiving only the most basic care, or none. The bigger animals are expected to "perform." If they don't do what they've been trained to do, they are beaten. It's common for them to die from heat while being transported, or from malnutrition. In that case, they simply get replaced. And the show goes on.

For the kids brought to watch, the message is clear: animals are there for their pleasure, like toys or other inanimate objects.

Animal abusers claim there's an educational dimension to what they do, but it's all about the money. We do not need to see animals up close to learn about them. On the contrary. They are best observed in their habitat, from a distance, respecting them in their space. If we want to know more details, we can read about them, or watch documentaries, without invading their world and disrupting their lives.

In February of 2019, we organized a big press conference on the steps of the Los Angeles City Hall. Why LA? For one, because our longtime ally, former Los Angeles City Councilmember Paul Koretz, was introducing a resolution supporting the bill. Second, it's easier to get celebrities to come out for a cause in LA than in Sacramento. And we had some really big names on our side for this battle.

PETA had a connection with actor Lucy Davis and arranged for her to speak at the conference. She was brilliant. On stage behind us, holding signs, were actors Pablo Azar, Daniella Monet, Kristin Bauer van Straten, and Juan Pablo Di Pace. Oscar-winner Joaquin Phoenix's appearance brought a lot of media attention. He was named PETA's Person of the Year that year. Attorney Lisa Bloom spoke passionately about her journey from a child who loved the circus but knew in her gut that there was something inhumane about it, to an informed adult who refused to perpetuate the cruelty. Once her own kids found out what happened behind the scenes, they were happy to learn about animals through books and videos, seeing them in their natural habitats, roaming free with their families and herds.

Lily Tomlin put her name behind the campaign early on as well. One of America's most beloved actors and comedians, Lily had been working for years to get Billy the elephant moved out of the LA Zoo and into a sanctuary. Billy has been kept for more than thirty years, alone, in an enclosure that's way too small for him. He's so

Saving wild animals from the cruelty of circuses takes a village. Heartfelt thanks to high-profile animal lovers like Joaquin Phoenix, Lucy Davis, and Lisa Bloom, who are always ready to help draw attention to these important issues.

overwhelmed with distress that he spends all day, every day, rocking back and forth.

Lily sent the most beautiful letter of support to Senator Hueso before the bill's first stop in the Senate Natural Resources and Water

Committee. She laid out the facts about what the words "performance" and "entertainment" are supposed to mean:

> I've been in the entertainment industry for decades, and I know the importance of listening to your audience. It's 2019, and Californians can no longer tolerate terrified animals kept captive, tormented, and forced to perform tricks. That's why I support SB 313, the Circus Cruelty Prevention Act.
>
> I love performing and couldn't imagine doing anything else—but when I step on set, it's my choice. Animals condemned to a life on the road with a circus have no say in their exploitation. Circuses continue to abuse elephants and other animals, subjecting them into a life of pain and soul-crushing captivity. These innocent animals are broken, physically and psychologically, and forced into a life that is completely unnatural to every fiber of their being. We are better than this. Animals deserve better than this.
>
> I am proud to see my state leading the charge in making the world a kinder place for animals. We were the first state to ban the sale of animal-tested cosmetics. We've banned the sale of fur in several of our largest cities, including Los Angeles and San Francisco. And now it's time to ban cruel, dangerous traveling wild animal acts in the state of California.
>
> We have the opportunity to lead the country in showing kindness and compassion to animals. So let's do it.

Honestly, I couldn't have said it better myself. She captured our mission so beautifully.

■ ■ ■

Despite all the star power in our camp, and the best efforts of our campaign, the pressure from the other side was intense. Credit where credit is due: The opposition was organized. Relentless. Effective. It mobilized immediately and massively. Dozens of people showed up at Senator Hueso's Sacramento office the day after he introduced the bill, and it was flooded with calls and emails. Predictably, they were mostly using the education argument. In their telling, all those shows where animals were getting used and abused were about conservation and outreach. They had the gall to insist that operators were subjected to rigorous annual inspections by the Animal and Plant Health Inspection Service, or APHIS. Remember, that's the notoriously understaffed arm of the USDA that is supposed to oversee animal health, animal welfare, and plant health across the whole country. Businesses that use animals only have to comply with the Animal Welfare Act, which affords laughable protections.

Basically, you can't intentionally kill healthy animals, but otherwise anything goes. I'm oversimplifying, but barely.

Senator Hueso caved pretty quickly. He had only said yes to getting wild animals out of circuses. Adding all acts that required the transportation of wild animals brought out all kinds of opposition. He saw the political writing on the wall.

At some point in March, we learned that labor unions were getting in on the action. Anyone who had any kind of job associated with hauling animals around for entertainment piled on. It felt like every day, we needed to carve out another exemption for some group or other. They were networking like crazy, too, inviting their industry friends to join the fray. Their argument was always the same: These shows are *educational.* People need to be right up in animals' faces to learn about them.

We had the truth on our side—the shows were solely about exploitation and profits—but it didn't matter. Even before the bill went to its very first committee hearing, we had to agree to two amendments. Almost everything but circuses was removed. Adding insult to injury, a carve-out was included for dogs and cats because one man had a dog and cat show. He actually lobbied lawmakers to get that exemption, explaining that his animals were really well cared for and got lots of treats. Bottom line: he said he wasn't in it for the money and his animals were doing just fine. Same lie as the rest of them. Some group that parades horses around got involved at the last minute, and we had to make an exception for equine shows too. It was exasperating, but we didn't have a choice.

Finally, there was a big debate about what qualified as a circus. We knew they wanted assurances that rodeos wouldn't be affected. That was painful. Rodeos are hotbeds of animal abuse. But they generate a lot of money for the people who put them on. Money means lobbyists pressuring lawmakers to ignore the animals' suffering, which they did here.

By the time it got through all the committees and both houses, the bill was similar to the one adopted by New Jersey and Hawaii the year before.

Circuses had been in the spotlight since Ringling Bros. closed in 2017. It was getting harder to defend the indefensible where they were concerned. In the case of our bill, the exploiters did a really good job protecting their interests in other areas, after which most dropped off at some point during the year. They had gotten what they wanted. So had we. SB 313 banned the use of bears, tigers, elephants, monkeys, or other wild animals in circuses in California.

We dreamed of stopping all exploitation in these traveling shows, but for the time being, saving wild animals from circuses was a big enough step in the right direction. We worked nonstop to get this legislation passed. It was an uphill battle every day. We never could have done it without PETA. They brought the science. The citations. The grassroots support they had spent decades earning and expanding.

■ ■ ■

Fast forward to today. Ringling Bros. has made a comeback—without animals. Its cruelty-based business model is gone forever thanks to PETA and all the activists who worked for more than three decades to shut down the abuse, including Senator Hueso and our team.

In 2018, Nabisco changed the packaging on its Barnum's Animal Crackers boxes after more than 115 years. Kids sitting down to a snack used to see lions, gorillas, polar bears, and elephants in boxcars on their way to the circus. The new packaging shows a zebra, an elephant, a lion, a giraffe, and a gorilla living free in their natural habitats. PETA led that charge too. It understands the importance of changing the way animals are depicted. If people don't give a second thought to seeing animals in cages and circuses on packaging, then they won't give it a second thought when they see it in real life. It becomes normalized. Changing the image people have of animals in their minds is a crucial focus of the animal rights movement.

Not all the news is good. Billy is still in the LA Zoo, alone, in the same enclosure that's too small for him. There's a sanctuary ready and waiting to welcome him. Several individuals have volunteered to pay for his safe transport. But the zoo won't release him.

As for SCIL, while we celebrate our victory with SB 313, we haven't forgotten the other animals that are still getting hauled around from place to place in cages, being used as money-making props.

CHAPTER 15

SAVING THEIR SKINS

"Judie, you'll never believe what I'm looking at. A stingray wallet! It's 2018, and they're still selling wallets made from stingray skin!"

Dr. Michelson was on a ski trip with his family in Mammoth Mountain when he made this gruesome discovery in a local gift shop. We'd been working together on animal issues for a dozen years by this point.

"Have you ever seen a stingray up close? Do you know how beautiful they are?"

He texted me a video of a stingray. I saw what he meant. They are incredible creatures.

Remember, Dr. Michelson had risked getting kicked out of medical school because he refused to do research on animals. Forty years later, having amassed a fortune as a spinal surgeon and inventor with more than 953 patents around the world (issued or pending) as I write, he was devoting his time and wealth to causes that benefited people, animals, and the planet. Looking at that wallet that day, and knowing that a stingray had been killed to make it, he felt compelled to do something. And he knew who to ask.

"We need to make this illegal," he said.

"I agree," I said. "Let's look at it for 2020."

"Let's do it now."

Presto. SCIL's list of sponsored bills for the 2019 session had grown again.

■ ■ ■

California had long banned sales of products made from the skins of some endangered animals, while leaving others unprotected. It was all part of the ongoing, epic battle between breeders, hunters, and the fashion industry—which charges exorbitant amounts for wallets, belts, shoes, and other vanity items made from exotic skins—and those of us who know animals are sentient beings that don't deserve to be slaughtered to make clothing or accessories.

As willing as some lawmakers had said they were to carry an animal bill for us after all our successes, we weren't sure we could find an author for this one. Fisheries are big business in California. Sharks and stingrays are part of their business model. We knew opponents would come out swinging.

Assemblymember Brian Maienschein stepped up to the plate. He is a great animal lover and has been a huge ally for SCIL to this day. In 2019, he carried two bills for us: one banning sales of products made with exotic skins and our Transparency in Research Act, which aimed to protect the animals used in experiments in more than three hundred laboratories in California. That second bill got tabled, but the issue was picked up in 2023 by another group, with our support. Unfortunately, the final bill was partially watered down, but it did pass, and thus moved the needle forward.

When Assemblymember Maienschein introduced Assembly Bill 1260, Sales Ban on Exotic Skins, the list of threatened or endangered animals whose skins could not be sold in California notably included big cats, polar bears, dolphins, pythons, kangaroos, and whales. Our initial plan was to add hippos and a variety of reptiles to the list, as well as sharks and stingrays. A poll we commissioned in January 2019 showed that a full 75 percent of Californians favored a ban, with 84 percent strongly supporting it. These were huge numbers. An overwhelming majority of Californians didn't want products made from these animals' skins sold in their state.

Assemblymember Maienschein laid out the issue in the clearest terms possible. "Maybe there was a time when our ancestors needed to wear the skin from a stingray or of a hippopotamus, but that time is long gone. These are fashion choices, plain and simple, and they are destroying biodiversity around the world." It's true. In the end, it all comes down to consumers' willingness to sacrifice biodiversity to achieve a certain look. To buy from companies that skin animals alive or use third-party vendors that do so in order to feel fashionable or wealthy or whatever it is those items of clothing make them feel.

Let's face it: wearing clothes or accessories made from animal skins makes a statement about your worldview, not your taste.

We had seen positive movement in the fashion industry already. Stella McCartney summed up the whole issue as well as anyone could: "There's nothing fashionable about a dead animal that has been cruelly killed just because some people think it looks cool to wear." Her brand and others were dedicated to selling only cruelty-free fashion. Actor and producer Louise Linton, a longtime advocate for animals and wildlife and SCIL board member since 2019, released her own line of vegan high heels in 2022. Her company donates 5 percent of proceeds to environmental welfare and conservation and plants a tree for every pair sold.

There have never been more options than today to look good while doing good.

Back in 2019, a number of international brands like Chanel, H&M, Hugo Boss, Nike, Puma, and Victoria's Secret, among many others, had adopted policies forbidding the use of exotic animal skins. Awareness was growing that killing animals for their skins is unnecessary and wrong. Most consumers don't want to have any part of that inhumane enterprise.

SCIL was the official sponsor of AB 1260, but once again, PETA did everything it could to help behind the scenes. PETA President Ingrid Newkirk gave us a statement of support and mobilized the troops via social media to get activists to Sacramento for the first

Assemblymember Brian Maienschein, me, and Nick Sackett finish our testimony for AB 1260, then enjoy listening to all the animal lovers who came to support it.

hearing in April. Ingrid is someone who has consistently backed SCIL with conviction and generosity.

■ ■ ■

Reality hit us pretty quickly. The only registered opposition when the bill went into the first committee was the Pacific Coast Federation of Fishermen's Associations. Just one group, but it represented fishing interests up and down the coast. As we anticipated, it focused on the shark and stingray fisheries in California and federal waters adjacent to the state, saying they were managed sustainably and subject to "extensive and severe" enforcement. Additionally, it warned that preemption issues would arise if a state law interfered with commercial fishing practices permitted by federal agencies.

The strikeouts suggested in the bill analysis from that first committee meeting told the whole story:

The committee may wish to consider an amendment removing sharks and stingrays from the list of animals included in the ban. Specifically, the amendment strikes the words shark and stingray on page 2 in line 24:

"[. . .] the dead body, or any part or product thereof, of an iguana, skink, caiman, shark, stingray, hippopotamus, or a Teju, Ring, or Nile lizard."

Already, the opposition was narrowing the scope of the bill as much as it could. Realistically, we knew we didn't stand a chance taking on the fisheries, especially if we were setting up a showdown between federal and state agencies. A bill that could create that kind of conflict was a nonstarter. As devastating as it was, the sharks and stingrays were removed from the bill. Once again, we'd take the opportunity to save some animals now and hopefully come back for others later. Pragmatism is important. Without it, we're just another group of animal rights activists.

In the end, AB 1260 added seven species—iguana, skink, caiman, hippos, and three types of lizards—to the list of animals whose bodies could not be used in products sold in California starting in 2022.

■ ■ ■

Notably missing from AB 1260 were alligators and crocodiles. The reason was simple: California had banned sales of products made from the skins of those animals back in 1970. Under pressure from breeders, hunters, the meat and hide industry, and the state of Louisiana, in 2006, the legislature passed, and Governor Arnold Schwarzenegger approved a temporary exemption lasting in theory until 2010. It was extended in 2009 due to lobbying by the same parties. Then again in 2014. Each time, lawmakers included a sunset date. The exemption adopted in 2014 was set to expire on January 1, 2020, which was coming up fast.

Attitudes had changed in the interim. More people had become aware of the disgusting and cruel way these animals are bred and slaughtered, and wanted to make sure they weren't supporting the industries behind the suffering. For the first time, we were confident that, armed with the facts, lawmakers would finally take a courageous stand against special interests and toss the exemption into the dustbin of history, where it belonged.

Those special interests were determined, though, and flush with cash. To defeat the attempts to extend the exemption again, we'd have to go to the mat for every vote.

Fortunately, SCIL was a well-oiled machine that year. Nick was up to speed and ready to manage the policy side of things—the actual writing of bills—with our partners. That freed up more time for me to do public relations. Experts from PETA and the Center for Biological Diversity (CBD) gave us the content we needed to go door to door in the Capitol and explain what the opponent's bills would really do and refute the falsities they were pushing.

The task of putting information together in a way that is comprehensive and tells a compelling story is monumental. PCRM, CBD, and PETA do it best.

On February 14, Assemblymember Randy Voepel, a Republican from Santee, introduced Assembly Bill 527, Import, Sale or Possession of Wildlife. In its original version, it would have simply eliminated a provision in existing law that extended the ban on sales of crocodile and alligator products, officially making it legal to sell them in California again. The arguments were that alligators weren't endangered anymore and that the industry was well-regulated and not doing any harm to anyone.

The forces behind the bill quickly came to understand that this iteration—a simple repeal of the ban—didn't have a chance of making it through the legislature. So the author amended it by pushing back the sunset date. That had worked well for decades, why not try it again? Kicking the can further down the road would keep the profit machine going. When the new AB 527 went to its first hearing in the Assembly Water, Parks and Wildlife Committee in early April, it called for the exemption to be extended through January 1, 2030. Ten more years of profits for the exploiters—another ten years of torture and death for the alligators.

Odds were this wasn't going to fly, either. Lawmakers knew where voters stood on the issue. But the exploiters weren't going to let public opinion get in their way. They never did. Their thinking is aim high, bargain your way down, and grab the money while it's there. That's how they operate. Animals are collateral damage on their march toward bigger profits.

Before a committee or floor vote, lawmakers consult what's called the bill analysis. Prepared by committee consultants, the analysis lays out what existing law says, how the bill would change it, and what the fiscal effects of the change would be. Background information about the issue is included, along with details of current and prior related legislation. At the bottom are summaries of proponents' and opponents' arguments for and against the bill, followed by the list of registered support and opposition. The names at the bottom of the analysis—those who support and oppose the bill—are often the first thing lawmakers look at. Knowing who's behind a bill, and who's fighting it, can tell them more about the legislation they're considering than the text itself. An assemblymember once said publicly that our name is the first thing she checks for on an animal bill. "Whatever side SCIL is on is the right side," she said. That's one of the highest compliments we've ever received. We would love for more legislators to follow her lead.

Before AB 527's first committee hearing, nine groups had signed on to oppose it, including SCIL, PETA, CBD, and NRDC. A total of 624 individuals sent letters. On the other side, the list of official support was almost seventy names long. Members of Congress from Louisiana, including both US senators from that state. Agencies from Alabama and Mississippi. Farmers' associations from Zambia and Zimbabwe. Retail associations, business federations, leather goods companies. Even the Federation of the Swiss Watch Industry chimed in. The exploiter network was working overtime, roping in as many companies and organizations as possible to extend the sunset date.

The driving force behind all this support was the Louisiana Alligator Advisory Council. A division of the Louisiana Department of Wildlife and Fisheries, the council's official mission is to "support Louisiana's wild alligator population through ranching and sustainable use programs." What it actually does is lobby for the groups that make money off alligators or kill them for sport. We're talking serious money. You can go online today and buy a second-hand Hermès Birkin bag, made from baby alligators, for $250,000. The titans of the fashion industry were fighting us from the shadows, letting the council do their bidding. It wasn't hard to imagine that if they had their way, these animals would be exempted from every anti-wildlife trade law.

For this fight, the council kept its lobbyists working overtime in the Capitol, pressuring lawmakers, showering money on them, and keeping up a steady drumbeat on social media. The message was clear: The alligator killers were the good guys. They were saving animals, habitats, jobs. We were naïve, crazy animal rights activists who knew nothing about how the economy worked and refused to acknowledge how good those animals had it.

Of all the David and Goliath battles I've been involved in, this was probably the most daunting. It seemed like every time we turned around, a new group was registering to support the anti-alligator legislation of the week. Initially, our biggest opponent was the state of Louisiana. No surprise there. And the big fashion houses, of course. Multinationals that have so much cash they don't know what to do with it. One way to spend it is to deploy lobbyists to help pass laws they call pro-business, but that are in fact anti-animal. Anything to keep selling expensive wallets and shoes made from tortured animals.

They also give money to lawmakers who they know will vote against animal rights bills. Lots of it. I can tell you that in 2019, the money was flowing into the coffers of anyone who'd side with the exploiters. They even tried to buy us off in the basement of the Capitol with an offer to run a conservation fund endowed with a million dollars. All we had to do was let AB 527 get through. Give the exploiters free rein to keep killing as many alligators as they wanted.

Besides the ethical reasons for opposing the bill, we had to challenge the ridiculous promise its author made that only legally traded products would be allowed into the state. While American alligators had made a spectacular comeback thanks to the Endangered Species Act and other protections, research showed that most of the illegally traded wildlife products seized were made from wild crocodiles and caimans sourced in other countries. Our opponents invented an insane story about how a disclosure system would make it possible to track and trace every product sold in California. According to them, consumers would be able to confidently buy alligator and crocodile goods knowing that no international treaties were violated in their production. It was pure fantasy. There was no feasible way to know where products came from. Not to mention that legally traded animals suffered immensely too. These "cruelty-free farms" the exploiters kept talking about didn't exist. There's no humane way to skin an animal alive.

On April 22, the author amended the bill to add in the meaningless disclosure promise.

A new version, with the new disclosure provision and still extending the sunset to 2030, was sent to Assembly Appropriations on May 1. That committee was chaired by Assemblymember Lorena Gonzalez, who was carrying the fur trapping ban for us that year.

An animal lover through and through, she had her finger on the pulse of California voters.

The job of Appropriations is to determine the fiscal effect of a bill. With the new disclosure requirement, cost was a legitimate concern. How many people would the Department of Fish and Wildlife (DFW) need to hire to enforce this magical disclosure provision? As the committee pointed out, when California banned sales of elephant tusks and rhinoceros horns in 2015, enforcement costs were estimated at a million dollars a year, and DFW ended up having to hire ten additional wardens. How would the new costs be covered?

Chair Gonzalez was not buying what these snake oil salesmen were selling and the opposition knew it. They had to find a way to get around her.

The bill was scheduled for another hearing in May, but the author postponed it. Indefinitely, as it turned out—he knew the votes weren't there. It was the end of the road for AB 527, but not for the effort to extend the exemption.

■ ■ ■

"Gut and amend" is when an author finds a bill that's already passed one house, empties it of all its contents (guts it), and puts in entirely different provisions through amendments. The bill then resumes its forward march with new content, but without the public review opportunities that are supposed to occur along the way. Used in Sacramento for over a century, it's a controversial practice, as the new language may be totally unrelated to the original text.

Some justifications for gut and amends sound reasonable. Deadlines for introducing legislation and getting it through committee and floor votes are fairly tight. Once you fall behind, it can be hard to catch up. The ability to transfer the content of a bill into a new vehicle that is not serving any other purpose can be a useful tool.

But sometimes it's simply a bait-and-switch tactic. Your bill dies because it doesn't have enough support. You find one that's idling in a committee somewhere and stuff your own provisions into it, hoping you'll get more traction with the new vehicle. It also leaves less time for opponents to figure out what's happening and organize a response.

We put this thought-provoking billboard on the on-ramp to the freeway legislators have to take to get to the Sacramento airport.

In the case of the legislators working to keep sales of alligator hide products legal, it was a bait-and-switch.

Assembly Bill 719 had been introduced on February 19, 2019 by a Republican lawmaker from Orange County. It called for part of California's $21 billion budget surplus to be used to shore up the state's struggling public health insurance program. After making it through two committees and an Assembly floor vote, the bill was on hold, making it a perfect vessel to use for our opponents. On June 20, AB 719 got a new name—Endangered Wildlife, Crocodiles and Alligators—and a new purpose. Other than the sunset date being moved up from 2030 to 2025 to make it seem more reasonable, it was essentially identical to AB 527.

Special interests from Louisiana were splashing so much money around that multiple lawmakers agreed to sign on as coauthors.

The newly gutted and amended AB 719 had its first committee hearing in the Senate on July 9. Our opponents were giving it their all. Various groups operated in the background, organizing support online and clamoring about their rights—shoppers' rights, retailers' rights, hunters' rights. Everybody had rights except the alligators and crocodiles. Even dog food makers were in on it now, whining about how their whole industry would be disrupted. We looked and looked and found only one dog food brand made with alligator meat.

The constant onslaught was exhausting. Our opponents had so much money, especially the high fashion houses. They shape-shifted constantly. One group would go quiet for a while, then reemerge in a different hearing with a different name. It was chaotic, time-sucking, and infuriating.

At one point, we noticed some new names on the support list: biomedical companies. What on earth?

As we soon discovered, the opposition had manufactured claims that alligators were widely used in research, that all kinds of new miracle drugs being developed for humans using antibodies from alligators were just about to reach the market. They said people from California would miss out on these drugs if alligator products were banned. The main lobbyist was going around the Capitol telling a sob story about how these alligator tests were key to finding a cure for a disease afflicting one of his children. The dishonesty was breathtaking. To see a lobbyist exploiting his own child's illness to further the interests of his clients disgusted everyone on our side. Alligator antibodies were *not* being used in medical research. These stories were being pulled out of thin air.

Dr. Michelson was furious when he heard about this new antibody research argument. As an animal lover. As a scientist and inventor. As a person of impeccable integrity. He issued an epic response:

> *Louisiana special interests hypothesizing that alligator antibodies working for alligators would be a new miracle drug for use in humans is disingenuous at best. There is no citation of even a single drug derived from alligators. Economically motivated speculation and commercial propaganda that flies in the face of the actual science in regard to the prospects of inter-species antibody transfers should be seen exactly for that—as speculation and propaganda. And if the day ever arrives when an FDA-approved drug derived from alligators comes to market, federal law would preempt state law and thus allow the sale of any FDA-approved drugs in California.*

Facts.

No matter how many angles of attack they found and how many random groups they had on their side, we went toe to toe with them. Our lobbyists and supporters were in every hearing, every meeting, every hallway. By now, lawmakers understood that their votes on animal bills would be scrutinized and affect their public image as well as their elections. Most of them were willing to hear the truth. Eventually, most would do the right thing.

Seeing the writing on the wall, in June, the Louisiana lobby found someone to try yet one more gut and amend. One last Hail Mary.

This time, the coauthors and witnesses for the bill laid out the usual smorgasbord of lies about all the medical research that was being conducted on alligators in California universities, all the wetlands that were benefiting from conservation efforts in the southeastern United States, not to mention that wetlands capture carbon, so there was a climate change angle too. I was rolling my eyes so hard.

The point they made about alligators not being endangered anymore was partly true. But they were cherry-picking their data. In its opposition testimony, Defenders of Wildlife pointed out that while *American* alligators had made a comeback thanks to the Federal Endangered Species Act and other protections, in other parts of the world, wild crocodiles, alligators, and caimans weren't faring so well. Illegal trade was booming. Banning the sale of products made from alligator and crocodile skins was the only way to stop California from contributing to it.

Nick was the second witness in opposition during the Senate Natural Resources and Water Committee hearing on the bill. After clarifying that international law offers no protections at all in terms of how animals are killed, he gave members of that committee an excruciating, graphic description of all the kinds of torture and suffering these alligators endure.

Over a hundred people went to the microphone as add-ons. They just kept coming. A few said they had walked 150 miles from San Francisco to speak that day to get their opposition on the record.

And yet the bill passed the committee, which scared us. A few of our allies had gone over to the dark side. Some of their staffers were furious with them, as I later learned. One lawmaker who we thought was a big wildlife guy bought into all the nonsense about the benefits of alligator breeding, all the natural habitat that had been preserved, all the medical research, all the small businesses that would close if they couldn't keep selling alligator boots and wallets.

When the bill passed that committee, it was on the strength of extraordinary promises made by our opponents about amendments to come. The sunset period could be shortened to light a fire under the industry and force it to act quickly. A legislative review would be scheduled. Fish and Wildlife would have a mandate. The list went on. All kinds of fantasies were being tossed around when the bill was adopted and sent to the Appropriations suspense file.

On August 30, Dr. Michelson, Diane Keaton, Maggie Q, and I wrote an op-ed that was posted to Patch, summing up the debate in the most concise terms possible. We placed the crocodile and alligator issue within a broader context of sustained attacks on wildlife preservation across the country under the Trump administration. Legal sales were a cover for illegal sales, and there was no track and trace system that could ever stop it. We chose to run it on that day because it was the deadline for the bill to be pulled off the suspense file.

At midnight, we breathed a huge sigh of relief. AB 719 was dead. Speaker Anthony Rendon and Chair Gonzalez had the moral conviction to stand by us and allow the bill to go to its final resting place. They are from the rare class of politicians who can be counted on to do the right thing for the right reasons. I've known a few who voted against a good bill or supported a bad one because they truly misunderstood what they were voting on. Animal exploiters are nothing if not convincing. But mostly, weak politicians vote for or against bills based on the prospect of money and influence. And they use the animal exploiters' arguments to give them cover.

That's how propaganda is supposed to work. And it works really well in Sacramento.

Once in a while, SCIL sends out an email telling our followers that we've made history. The day we announced the defeat of the alligator bill, we meant it. But we knew it was just a temporary reprieve. Nick's ominous statement said it all: "This is not the last we've heard from the alligator and high fashion industries. We expect they'll be back in January, and we'll be here waiting for them."

He was right. The exploiters do come back. Year after year. And we are here waiting for them.

EPILOGUE

In November 2019, I got a call from local journalist Brooke Staggs informing me that she'd like to do a feature on me for the *Orange County Register.* I agreed on the condition that she tell me more about the piece she was planning. The *Register* is very conservative, so it's not always aligned with my politics. I never imagined that I was to be included in its annual list of the hundred most influential people in Orange County. Much less that I was in the top ten.

Titled "If Animals Could Vote, Judie Mancuso Would Be President," the feature ran on December 23. It captured all the victories and heartbreaks of 2019, and SCIL's determination to use the momentum we'd gained to get big things done at the state and national levels in 2020. These included a federal law to prevent international puppy mills from selling dogs in the US. Multiple bills to benefit wildlife, endangered species, horses at racetracks, and of course, dogs and cats. We were going to help dairy and animal farmers at risk of losing their livelihoods build robust and sustainable new businesses centered on plant-based proteins. And we were going to take care of all that unfinished business—protect the stingrays that got left out of our exotic skins bill, ban imports of animal trophies from Africa for good, and stop out-of-state puppy mills from skirting California's new law we sponsored.

Great things were on the horizon. We could feel it.

Margie Perenchio hosted a giant fundraiser for SCIL at the Bel-Air Country Club on February 1, 2020. We honored Assemblymembers Lorena Gonzalez and Ash Kalra and celebrated our new board members, Diane Keaton and Louise Linton.

With all those big plans, we were going to need big money. Our supporters came through once again, ensuring that we'd be ready to hit the ground running. As soon as the legislature was back in session, Nick and I started working seven days a week to lay the groundwork for more big successes.

All of SCIL's board members, including Diane Keaton, honoring Assemblymembers Lorena Gonzalez and Ash Kalra at our 2019 fundraiser.

There were already murmurings about a few cases of a new flu going around. We had no idea a huge boulder was thundering down the hill, heading straight toward us.

By the end of March 2020, COVID-19 had effectively shut the Capitol down. Committee chairs were drawing a red line through any bills they didn't view as COVID-19-related. Personal protective equipment and stimulus payments were in; bold action to protect animals and the planet was out.

Of the nine SCIL-sponsored bills that already had bill numbers, seven got tabled. All those relationships we'd spent years cultivating changed dramatically. No more dropping by lawmakers' offices to go over the details of a bill with them or their staff. Everything went online. Our calls and emails started going unanswered as all the energy and resources shifted to the pandemic.

Fundraising ground to a halt too. Donors had no idea when we were going to be able to resume our work in earnest, plus they had their own economic uncertainty to deal with. A totally unexpected windfall came late in 2020 when Steven Bernheim, the man who'd written SCIL its first check ever, arranged to have a considerable amount of money donated to SCIL from a class action lawsuit settlement fund. That money gave us the ability to continue our work during the pandemic. It kept us going when there were very little other funds coming in.

■ ■ ■

On January 6, 2021, insurrectionists stormed the US Capitol to overturn the results of the 2020 presidential election. COVID-19 had already caused some partisanship to creep into the SCIL board. Until then, I had been able to bring together animal lovers from different political persuasions and unite them around the cause. But suddenly, board members were arguing with me and one another on social media about mask mandates. Vaccines. Voter fraud. Democracy itself. For the first time, it became impossible to keep the focus of all discussions among board members on the animals. Everything became political.

Early in February 2022, a call came in on my cell phone from a New York area code. It was Tucker Carlson's scheduler, asking if I'd go on the show to talk about the Dog and Cat Bill of Rights we were sponsoring that year. In seven broad clauses, it covered everything from the right to live free from cruelty and neglect to the right to daily food, water, shelter, mental stimulation, and appropriate exercise. Had it passed, all public animal control agencies and shelters, SPCA and humane society shelters, and rescue groups would have been required to post the bill of rights in their facilities or on their websites, to remind potential adopters that the animals they were coming to meet or take home had rights.

The scheduler promised me that Carlson was an animal lover and that his goal in having me on was to talk about that bill.

My first reaction was to say no. Fox News had been pretty fair to me in the past, but I loathed what it had come to represent, and honestly viewed it as a threat to American democracy. (I still do.) I was clear with the scheduler that I didn't watch the show and fully expected Carlson to hijack the segment and make it about something else. She assured me that wouldn't happen. He just wanted to talk about that one bill.

It was a real moral dilemma for me. I sought advice from lawmakers, fellow animal rights advocates, and friends. A few warned me not to do it, saying Carlson was too divisive and toxic and that he'd end up attacking or making fun of me. I wasn't really worried about that. He did seem to be a proponent for animals. But was he planning to ambush me to rile up his viewers? The last call I made was to our friend Kathy Guillermo, vice president at PETA, who'd been on Carlson's show several times. She confirmed that he was an animal guy and reminded me that even if he weren't, I couldn't turn down an opportunity to get in front of an audience of four to six million people to speak for the animals.

Still filled with apprehension, I agreed to appear on the show on a Friday. On Thursday, Putin invaded Ukraine. Our segment got bumped for several months, during which time I watched Carlson spout pro-Russia conspiracy theories and other nonsense. Grateful not to be associated with the host in any way, I had written the whole thing off. Until the scheduler called back in May, saying she hadn't forgotten about me and could I come on the following week?

No, I said, absolutely not. I'm appalled by Carlson's sympathy for Russia. She assured me that was not the case, and that he just wanted to talk about the bill.

With even more dread than the first time, I accepted, for the sake of the animals.

To my horror, Carlson kicked off the segment with an insane rant about Dr. Anthony Fauci funding experiments on beagles. It was one of those contorted stories that Fox takes out of context to stir up controversy. Dr. Fauci was head of the National Institute of Allergy and Infectious Diseases, part of the National Institutes of Health. The NIH had funded animal testing under the leadership of all its directors, which I and other animal rights defenders staunchly oppose. But Dr. Fauci was leading the government response to COVID-19, and Fox was leading the opposition to it. Carlson was only bringing up the issue to fire up the outrage machine and undermine a Democratic administration.

He started by saying, "Judie, thanks so much for coming on. Tell us how you could stop this."

Exactly the bait-and-switch I had feared. He wanted me to use our bill to join him in attacking Dr. Fauci. Instead, I launched straight into my explanation of what the Dog and Cat Bill of Rights would do and why it was necessary. I talked about how we had banned the sale of animal-tested cosmetics in California and would love to do more to end taxpayer-funded animal testing in general.

Carlson did everything he could to get me to join him in Fauci-bashing, but I kept the conversation on track.

To his credit, he ended by thanking me, and noting that if you mistreat dogs, you will mistreat people. That is a true statement, and it's something that can't be repeated enough.

Unsure how SCIL supporters would react to me going on the show, I sent out an email blast to provide context and explain why I accepted the invitation. That statement ended up getting more pushback than the appearance itself. One longtime supporter, a major donor and board member, expressed her disappointment that I felt the need to apologize for going on Fox News when I should have felt honored. Within a year's time, she and another member would leave the board.

Trump, COVID-19, January 6, and the war in Ukraine were driving a wedge deep into a nonprofit board that had always been a refuge from partisan politics.

■ ■ ■

I have been asked why I decided to run for State Assembly in 2022. The most immediate reason was that otherwise, a right-wing Republican with no regard for the truth, the environment, or women's rights would have been on the ballot unopposed. I was encouraged by many Democrats to jump into the race, and I did, but not solely out of party loyalty. I believe in representative democracy and want the people in my district to have a genuine voice in Sacramento. Needless to say, another benefit of winning would have been the ability to introduce truly bold bills to protect animals and the environment, the kind of legislation some lawmakers are still too fearful to take on because it might cost them support from special interests. Or maybe they just don't want to be bothered with anything that rocks their boat.

Priscilla Presley is one of the most gracious people I have met. She posed for photos with everyone who asked. Shown here with Nick Sackett, Simone Reyes, me, and Dr. Gary Michelson.

We honored Assemblymembers Wendy Carrillo and Marie Waldron for being committed pro-animal legislators.

People still come up to me today to say how sorry they are that I lost. To which I say, it was one of the greatest experiences of my life, and I have no regrets. The work I did during that campaign broadened my advocacy in ways I could have never imagined. It made my world bigger, starting with all the smart, hard-working, engaged, and engaging people

ACR 86, our Pet Crisis Response Act, got a big boost from American icon Priscilla Presley. During a trip to Sacramento to advocate for the resolution, she posed (above) with Senator Rosilicie Ochoa Bogh, Nick Sackett, me, Assemblymembers Ash Kalra and Marie Waldron, Kenn Altine, and Simone Reyes.

I connected with. The conversations I had with voters gave me invaluable insight into how people live and what they really care about. I can confirm that Orange County is chock-full of animal lovers. People who care deeply about pets, wildlife, and marine life and want to see them protected.

Steven Bernheim and Dr. Gary Michelson, pictured here at our July 2023 fundraiser at Dr. Michelson's home with me and Steven's friend. They have been the pillars of SCIL's existence since the beginning.

■ ■ ■

On a warm evening in July 2023, SCIL friends and supporters gathered in the Brentwood home of Alya and Dr. Gary Michelson for our first fundraiser since COVID-19. We gave awards to Assemblymembers Marie Waldron and Wendy Carrillo for supporting pro-animal legislation. And we honored a truly special guest, American icon Priscilla Presley, for her life's work saving and protecting animals.

Like so many wonderful things that have happened to SCIL, Priscilla got connected with us by chance. Simone Reyes was calling everyone she knew to find a foster home for a sweet dog. She reached out to a rescuer who, over the course of the conversation, mentioned that he had worked with Priscilla on an effort to save a dog. Never one to be shy about connecting animal lovers with SCIL, Simone asked if her friend could mention our organization to Priscilla.

Within a few days, we were coordinating Priscilla's public support for Assembly Concurrent Resolution 86, a SCIL-sponsored resolution designed to get California to direct new resources toward resolving the dramatic overpopulation crisis in state shelters that had been sharply exacerbated by COVID-19.

That fundraiser was like a homecoming for many of us, after years of being kept apart by the pandemic. There were also a lot of new faces there, particularly young attorneys who are interested in seeing new laws passed that will save and protect animals.

When we had all caught up on conversation, feasted on vegan food, and properly celebrated our awardees, longtime supporter Steven Bernheim stood up, pulled a check from his wallet, and carefully, slowly unfolded it before the crowd. He said, "I'm going to kick us off with this contribution. Who's going to match me?" It was like being back in 2007. Starting fresh, but with years of experience and success behind us. And with an army of friends who share my determination to create a more compassionate world for all people and all animals.

My phone always rings constantly the day after an event. When I answered the first call the next morning, I never expected to hear Priscilla's voice. She just wanted to say how much she felt at home at our event. Like she was among family, with people who share her deep desire to live in a more compassionate world.

I told her that's exactly what SCIL is about. Bringing the biggest family possible together on this planet Earth we call home to protect and care for one another, including the animals that need us to be their voice.

On we go.

ACKNOWLEDGMENTS

People had been telling me for years that I needed to write a book about my life. It wasn't until I met Jennifer McDonald in 2022 that I started to believe that project could become a reality. I quickly realized Jennifer could convey the spirit of compassion that drives me. She helped me tell my story in a way that puts the focus where it belongs: on the animals, what it takes to save and protect them, one law at a time, and the people who make our work possible.

I mention in this book some of the folks who played high-profile roles at crucial times to help SCIL pass landmark laws. It was impossible to weave into the stories the name of every person who assisted us by providing financial, logistical, policy-writing, political, lobbying, organizational, and moral support. Nor could I name all the compassionate elected officials, staff members, celebrities, performers, rescuers, volunteers, donors, and other animal advocates who stepped up when we needed them.

There is another group of people I cannot thank individually because there are too many of you, often operating anonymously: I am referring to the thousands of SCIL supporters who, since 2007, have been answering calls to action for the animals month after month, year after year; those who come to Capitol hearings or local government meetings to give testimony and speak in support of our efforts; and those who contact lawmakers to urge them to support pro-animal legislation. Thank you all, and please keep it up. After all these years working closely with people in government, I can assure you that your calls, your emails, your testimonies do make a difference.

Below is a list of some of the people whose names came up or came to mind while retracing SCIL's history to write this book. If your name is not on the list but should be, know that I carry you in my heart.

Kenn Altine, Bob Alvarez, Wendy Aragon, Bob Aragon, Amitis Ariano, Sabrina Ashjian, Shira Astrof, Diane Babcock, Josh Balk, Gini Barrett, Geoff Baum, Gene Baur, Garry Beers, Jourdan Beers, Shelly Bennecke, Roseryn Bhudsabourg, Jim Bickhart, Bob Blumenfield, Keith Bohr, Lani Bray, Aaron Brieno, Mina Brown, Taimie Bryant, Genelle Butler, Gloria Butler, Beth Caffrey, Kelly Carlson, Kim Carr, Lisa Carter, Pam Casselman, David Casselman, Zak Castillo-Krings, Jon Cicirelli, Jennifer Conrad, Baltazar Cornejo-Lujan, Karen Coyne, Sheila Creal, Bill Crowe, Samantha Crowe, Andrea Cunningham, Leslie Davies, Jenny Day, Betsy Denhart, Donna Dennison, Dr. Allan Drusys, Nigel Duarte, Matthew Duncan, Jeff Ebenstein, John Ehlers, Nancy Ehrlich, Shelley Elam, Michael Elam, Pablo Espinoza, Shanna Ezzell, Joy Falk, Randi Feilich, Bob Ferber, Holly Fraumeni De Jesus, Simone Friedman, Bill Gage, Jennifer Galehouse, Nilang Gor, Evelyn Gray, Lorrie Green,

Jim Greenbaum, Kirsten Gross, Ryan Guillen, Zena Hallak, Katharine Hampton, Jennifer Hanson, Bob Hartman, Ivanna Heard Giorgallides, Dr. Zarah Hedge, Nancy Heigl, Katherine Heigl, Lee Heller, Anna Herby, Erica Hughes, Valarie Ianniello, Liz Jacobelly, Marilyn Jasper, Jim Jensvold, Dr. Richard Johnson, Melya Kaplan, Lisa Karlin, Kate Karp, Danielle Katz, Rebecca Katz, Mark Kennedy, Michelle Kiely, Jim Kilby, Phil Kim, Dr. Paula Kislak, Bruce Krider, Ronnie Kudlow Steinau, Sal LaBarbera, Chela Landau, Cindy Landon, Lisa Lange, Ellen Lavinthal, Patrick Le, Aaron Leider, Gretchen Lieff, Mayra Lombera, Dr. Lorin Linder, Luigi Luciano, Michael Lucien, Sosan Madanat, John Mancuso, Mary Ann Mancuso, Howie Mandell, Deni Markuson, Barbara McDonald, Christy Means, Lauren Meister, Gil Michaels, Laurie Michaels, Brenda Mitchell, Tom Modica, Liz Monaco, Kacey Montoya, Katharine Moore, Daphna Nachminovitch, Ariel Nessel, Morgan Newton, Hunter Nolan, Brian Nowicki, Dr. Mark Nunez, Terri Nunn, Kevins Olds, Daniel Paden, Lu Parker, Alanna Pearl, Bryan Pease, Tanya Petrovna, Katie Pettibone, Braden Pollack, John Popoch, Jeff Prang, Dr. Heather Rally Webb, Aaron Reyes, Erin Riley-Carrasco, Kathy Riordan, Mona Rios, Erika Ritchie, Melanie Sadek, Erika Salazar, Jose Sandoval, Christy Schilling, Miyoko Schinner, Joel Schulman, Kian Schulman, Teri Sforza, Patty Shenker, Dr. Heather Shenkman, Jessica Sieferman, Kim Sill, Lacey Skulls, Pam Slater-Price, Chayton Steinmann, Stephanie Stevens, Angie Tate, Ian Thompson, Mark Thompson, Fauna Tomlinson, David Toro, Alex Tucciarone, Jill Tucker, Katarina Van Derham, Monique Viera-Huestis, Julie Waldroup, Sue Walshe, Kevin Walshe, Michele Walther, Dr. Cheryl Waterhouse, Gabriel Wildgen, Annie Winner, Vince Wong, Brett Yates.

Governor Gavin Newsom was gracious to meet with the SCIL team and Priscilla Presley to discuss our life-saving bills.

Bringing the fight for animals to the Capitol Rotunda.

Me and Nick celebrating a milestone for AB 485 with the passionate and committed San Diego crew.

Dave Navarro, formerly of Jane's Addiction and the Red Hot Chili Peppers and always a rock star for the animals, performed at our Compassion Rocks III fundraiser.

SCIL board members, including Diane Keaton and Maggie Q, at our 2019 annual fundraiser.

An A-list crew performed at our 2014 Compassion Rocks fundraiser at Dick Clark's Malibu Estate, known as Gulls Way. Left to right, Tod Burr, JD Fortune, me, Pierce Brosnan, Dr. Karen Halligan, Katie Cleary, INXS founding member Garry Beers, and Dr. Jim Jensvold.

Nancy and Katherine Heigl with the late Erika Brunson, all longtime SCIL supporters.

Me with the late Sam Simon, co-creator of *The Simpsons* and animal rights activist, advocating to free whales from captivity.

Me with Assemblymember Adrin Nazarian looking on as members of the public voice their support for plant-based meals in schools.

ABOUT THE AUTHOR

Judie Mancuso is the founder, CEO, and president of Social Compassion in Legislation, one of the leading animal rights nonprofit in California working to save and protect animals through public policy. Landmark laws sponsored by her group have been copied in many other states and inspired at least one other major country to change its animal testing requirements. Judie became a full-time advocate for animals in 2007 after a twenty-year career in information technology. She served on the California Veterinary Medical Board from 2010 to 2018 and on the Environmental Sustainability Committee of her hometown, Laguna Beach, from 2019 to 2024. Judie shares her home with her two dogs and four cats—all rescues, of course.